AP LANG. FOR STUDENTS
And Their Teachers

A No Nonsense Guide for AP English Language
and Composition Essay Writing

Eduardo Barreto

Copyright © 2018 Eduardo Barreto
All rights reserved.
ISBN: 9781981007561

DEDICATION

To my students, past and present: I know I have taught you plenty, but I have learned even more. Thank you for helping me understand the things I'm always trying to explain, and for making clear the many things I still have to understand.

CONTENTS

	Acknowledgments	i
1	Writing Beatitudes	6
2	A Word on Rhetorical Analysis	9
3	Writing Rhetorical Analysis Essays	29
4	Complete Rhetorical Analysis Essay Examples	52
5	A Word on Synthesis	74
6	Writing the Synthesis Essay	86
7	Complete Synthesis Essay Examples	96
8	A Word on Argumentation	118
9	Writing the Argumentative Essay	126
10	Complete Argumentative Essay Examples	151
11	Appendix	177

ACKNOWLEDGMENTS

The composition of this book is owed in innumerable ways to the efforts of family, friends, colleagues, and most of all, my students; I'd like to take a moment and name a few.

To my wife, who never read this book while it was in composition, and will likely never read it, thank you for giving me what proofreaders never will: a relentlessly loving and understanding push, a home I am deliriously happy to go to after work, and two beautiful children I am glad look like their mother. If I could ask for a better wife, I would, but I doubt they have made her; I also don't think they accept returns after 90 days.

To Deanne Getreu, my Department Head, sworn AP Lang. ally-blood-sister, and friend: thank you for entrusting me with this class, equipping me for the fray, and for fighting by my side. May we storm many castles together.

To Margie Flores, thank you for reading this book when it had no hope of becoming what it has; thank you for believing it could be what it is; thank you for insisting I believe in the ones to come. Thank you.

To my students, Ana, Armando, Caro, Caroline and Nathaniel, without whose help this book would've probably been published months ago, but without whose help, this book would certainly not be all that it has become. Thank you for the delay. You refused to accept nothing but the very best; I hope I have given it to you.

A WORD ON THIS GUIDE

This book condenses thorough research, and my own classroom practice, into a guide that provides practical and ready-to-use information, which is organized systematically and comprehensively, and is accompanied by a variety of student essay samples, as well as scored student essays - all to show, simply, how one teacher teaches his AP English Language and Composition class. Although this guide is especially tailored for students of the course who want extra help in becoming the best writers they can be, this concise, instructional manual, can be used by either the instructor of the class or by those who have the time and interest in instructing themselves. The sections of this text are designed for students, who want condensed information, that can help clarify their classwork or pacify their concerns about the material covered in the course. The information herein can be used by instructors, for all classroom purposes, such as handouts, worksheets, and curriculum advice and is especially ideal for instructors who want ideas on how to re-structure their class or want to freshen up their material and pedagogy for the upcoming year, or for those teaching this course for the first time, who may want some guidance.

To both, the teacher and the student, this guide will save you time and effort.

To the teacher: As it often happens to teachers, we find something interesting we'd like to try, and in the process, discover that in order to implement it successfully, we must tweak it, change it, and frankly, turn it into a completely different activity in order to meet the needs of our students. But as it (also) often happens, teachers wear too many hats, and the one of "curious researcher who wants to continue learning and bring that knowledge into the classroom" is the hat we get to wear the least, because of classroom and teaching demands. I get it.

To the student: The strains of the classroom make it difficult, for teachers as well as students, to invest in private reading of auxiliary texts. Most students who take this course are taking equally challenging courses (sometimes 3 or more), and the pressure of these courses' classwork and homework combined make it difficult for them to be fully invested in each one. It's been my experience that, while my students want to learn more about my course (outside of my class), wading through 500 (albeit useful) pages of information, exams, graphs and pictures of happy students, uncharacteristically smiling while studying is just too much for the average student. I get it.

To both, the teacher and the student, this guide will save you time and effort.

This guide is divided into three parts: A Word on Rhetorical Analysis, A Word on Synthesis and A Word on Argumentation. These sections represent the three types of essays that are tested on the AP English Language and Composition Exam. While there is no particular order to them, the order in which I present them is meant to help teachers structure their own class throughout the year.

The course is ordered in a way that each unit informs the subsequent unit, building towards argumentation. The first unit (Rhetorical Analysis) sharpens the students' analytical skills by preparing them to understand, analyze, and evaluate information. These skills are later transferable and applicable to the reading of multiple sources during the Synthesis unit, which can then turn into sophisticated arguments during the Argumentation unit. If I were to begin with an Argumentation unit, for instance, that disposition of argumentation is likely to carry into the Rhetorical unit, where the purpose is to evaluate the writer's ability to persuade, not argue one's own ideas. Beginning with an Argumentation unit may also affect the student's approach to the Synthesis unit, because the key to Synthesis is to have a "conversation" with the sources, on a specific topic and with a defined opinion. I place the Argumentation unit last because a good argument is complex, and requires the previous two units to succeed.

While the order of the sections in this book is important to format the class in (what has proven in my teaching experience) the most effective way to maximize student interest, commitment and performance, the thorough instructions within each section, the detailed explanations of each step of the writing process, the student essay samples provided and the professional commentary that accompanies it, make this guide a handy tool for a tough job.

Sincerely, I hope this guide works for you, as it has worked for me.

BASIC ASSUMPTIONS

This book is written for teachers and students who are aware of the course's expectations and exam requirements, and would like additional help with the material or want to go beyond what their class can offer.

This guide only covers the writing portion of the AP English Language and Composition exam (Rhetorical, Synthesis and Argumentation) because it is the most important part of the test (in my opinion), and it requires the most attention and practice. While the Multiple Choice section is important (and worth 45% of the exam), it often doesn't feel as important as the Essay section because the student will spend twice as much time writing as they will, bubbling answers, and more to the point, writing has no lettered options to choose from; writing demands creation from nothing. That's tough.

Having listed some of the expectations you can have from this book, I am going to assume that you know the following things about the AP English Language and Composition course:

1. There's an exam administered by the College Board (usually in early May).

2. The exam in divided in two parts:
    a. Multiple Choice 52 to 55 Questions. 1 Hour. Worth 45% of the Exam Score.
    b. 3 Free Response Questions (Synthesis, Rhetorical Analysis, Argument). 2 Hours, 15 Minutes (15-minute reading period for Synthesis). Worth 55% of Exam Score.

3. The Free Response Questions (FRQs) are graded on a scale of 0 to 9:

   a. Effective: 8
   b. Adequate: 6
   c. Inadequate: 4
   d. Little Success: 2

4. This site: https://apcentral.collegeboard.org/ has many resources which can aid in the understanding of the exam. In the following site, you can find years of Free Response Questions: https://apcentral.collegeboard.org/courses/ap-english-language-and-composition/exam?course=ap-english-language-and-composition

5. The passing score for the AP English Language and Composition exam is a 3 (out of 5), and doing so will earn the student credit for a college composition course. Some universities, however, require a 4 or better to award credit for a college composition course.

6. AP English Language and Composition focuses on Nonfiction primarily, while AP English Literature and Composition focuses on fiction. Thus, the essays presented in this guide will only use nonfiction pieces as analysis.

WRITING BEATITUDES

Before beginning the essay sections, here are my 7 fundamental tenets of writing; all writing recommendations in this book are rooted in these beatitudes.

Be Clear

Muddy sentences are the product of laziness. If the reader can't tell what you're saying, he's not a poor reader – you're a poor writer. It's been said before, "hard writing makes for easy reading." Work, so your readers don't have to. The reader should labor when considering the implications of your ideas, or when admiring the freshness of thought in your writing, not when reading a complicated sentence that uses too many adjectives and doesn't know when to end.

Be Direct

The key is to arrive at your point faster. The longer you take to make your point, the less interested the reader becomes. The length of the sentence isn't the concern; a direct sentence can be a lengthy sentence or a short sentence. What matters is to present the reader with fewer things to think about in one sentence, or in one paragraph. Otherwise, the reader will have to choose what to pay attention to, and in doing so, lose part of what you are trying to say.

Be Simple

Simplicity is crucial. Some writers use 100-dollar words in 20-dollar conversations, but the reader is always more impressed with your ideas, than with the ostentatious words you use to explain them. And to be simple is not to be plain; simplicity can be powerful in creating images that are memorable to the reader. The key is to be simple in your style of composition, not in the caliber of your ideas.

Be Sure

If you don't believe what you're saying, why should I? I don't care if you're right or wrong, but be sure. This is not the same as being certain, which implies complete confidence, possibly after having "ascertained" that your belief is correct. No. Surety is about honesty. Your writing should say, "I agree with myself." Your writing should never become a trap that ensnares your reader in a disingenuous argument, that proves them or others wrong. Prove yourself right, not others wrong. Demonstrate that you make sense. Present your ideas with sincerity. Be sure.

Be Organized

The most unoriginal essay will still earn an adequate grade if it is organized, as a reader will always find value in order. Disorganized essays happen when writers, analogously, "answer the math problem, but they don't show the work." While readers may be impressed with your conclusions, they would be more impressed if you'd left a trail of breadcrumbs for them to follow. Incidentally, arguments are always stronger when the writer walks the reader through the thinking process, step by step. So, organize your writing by having a clear beginning, middle and end.

Be Brief

Brevity isn't about saying less; it's about saying enough. This is always difficult in a first draft, but when revising your essay, look for words or phrases that you can cut from your writing. This approach must be surgical, so as not to cut anything organic or the writer's personality, but doing so will declutter your essay.

Be Interesting!

You are writing about a prompt that the AP Language College Board has distributed to the rest of the country. The strategies you're noticing, other people are noticing. Even on a smaller scale, your teacher likely has more than 30 students, writing about the same prompt at once. What can you say, that they aren't? Nothing. But the way you say it, the insight you offer, that's how your AP readers and your teacher will differentiate your essay from the rest. Say something interesting. Say something exciting. Say something cool. Be riveting! And the only way to be interesting is to be interested in what you're writing about.

A WORD ON RHETORICAL ANALYSIS

With every year, it has become painfully obvious that Rhetorical Analysis (done right) is the most difficult thing you can ask of students. With every Rhetorical essay they write, they try a different approach, and they think this time they definitely got it. And they don't. They get some of it, but not all of it. What they eventually learn is that writing a Rhetorical Analysis essay is a multifaceted task that requires an equally multifaceted implementation of skills.

What is Rhetorical Analysis?

Google will tell you that "Rhetorical" relates to "Rhetoric" and that "Rhetoric is the art of persuasion." Google will also tell you that "Analysis" is fundamentally, "a detailed examination." Together, they make "a detailed examination of the art of persuasion." But these definitions only offer a tenuous beginning into the world of Rhetorical Analysis.

Detailed Definition

Rhetorical Analysis is the examination and breakdown of a certain texts into parts (strategies or devices) – parts that are then compared and contrasted with each other, in order to demonstrate how those parts, holistically, achieve a certain purpose (the author's intended purpose), usually of a persuasive nature.

Comprehensive Definition

Analysis refers to the use of critical reading skills to break the text being analyzed into manageable "**parts**" that can be scrutinized for insight into the whole of the text. It's tricky, because the students should not analyze in isolation, since it may seem as if they're missing the bigger picture, but they must demonstrate a close reading of a text, and relate that close reading to the purpose or aim of the text. Thus, the balancing act of Rhetorical Analysis (R.A.) is to articulate **HOW** the author crafts **WHAT** the author wrote.

A rhetorical analysis is **not a summary** of a literary work or scholarly article, but you do have to summarize the text, enough to contextualize the conversation. Rhetorical analysis is **not reviewing the meaning** of a text, rather it is ascertaining the purpose of the text before evaluating its efficacy in the use of strategies and devices to accomplish such purpose.

The next few pages:
    1. Reading the Prompt
    2. Reading the Text
    3. Writing the Essay

But first, a look into what the Rhetorical Analysis question looks like.

A Look at the Rhetorical Analysis Question

AP ENGLISH LANGUAGE AND COMPOSITION SAMPLE
RESPONSE
Question 2
(Suggested time—40 minutes)

Context
This paragraph introduces the **prompt**. Here, you will learn the author's name (sometimes only the title of the text or publication), the genre of the text (could be a speech, a letter, an essay or an article), the year in which it takes place, the immediate audience of the piece, and lastly, **the purpose of the text**. Pay close attention to the language the prompt uses to present the purpose of the text because it will be useful in your interpretation of the text and in the presentation of your thesis.

Text
The following paragraphs present an **excerpt of the text** you are to analyze. This text could be as lengthy as a page and a half, and could be any of the aforementioned genres. If it is a speech, consider its audience and the appeals it uses to target them. If it is a letter, read carefully, so as not to miss the implicit dialogue that you're not privy to. If it is an essay or an article, consider the argument of the piece and the logic it uses to prove it. Of course, there's so much more to consider when analyzing the text provided (and such will be covered in the following pages), but the first step is to consider the genre; doing so, will help you determine what device to pay closer attention to, and what rhetorical approach to take when writing your essay.

READING THE PROMPT

AP ENGLISH LANGUAGE AND COMPOSITION SAMPLE RESPONSE
Question 2
(Suggested time—40 minutes)

The **speech** below is an excerpt from **President John F. Kennedy's** Moon Speech at Rice Stadium on **September 12, 1962**. This speech was announced before a special joint session of Congress and later presented **to the American people**, the dramatic and ambitious goal of sending an **American safely to the Moon** before the end of the decade. Read the passage carefully. Then, in a well-developed essay, analyze the rhetorical strategies that Kennedy uses to **explain the benefits of such an endeavor**. Support your analysis with specific references to the text.

....

When reading the prompt, the goal is to anticipate the possible features of the text, in order to read it with purpose:

Author: President John F. Kennedy
Year: 1962
Audience: The American people
Purpose: To justify why America should go to the moon
Topic: Space exploration
Genre: Speech. Understanding the genre can help anticipate the techniques the text may use.

Pay attention to the **task** of the prompt, because it will help you anticipate the purpose of the text and/or the strategies it will use.

What is the task?

Although the task of the prompt is intuitive, it is much more nuanced than it appears to be. The task is to "analyze the rhetorical strategies the writer uses to..." That is always the task:

> Identify the <u>purpose</u> of the text and the <u>strategies</u> used in the text to accomplish that purpose.

Both the **purpose and the strategies come from the text**, of course, so you have to read the text in its entirety. However, if you read the prompt carefully, you'll find indications of what the purpose might be.

At a Glance

"Explain the benefits of such an endeavor" doesn't reveal much about the text, but here are some things to note:

1. The prompt tells me that his speech was delivered to the American people, so I should <u>be aware of the audience he had in mind</u> when I read his speech, to better understand the success of his strategies.

2. I also notice that President John F. Kennedy wants to "explain the benefits of" his proposal, which tells me <u>he knows Americans may be reluctant</u>, unless they understand what they can gain from it.

3. Lastly, the prompt tells me that the speech had the "dramatic and ambitious goal of sending an American safely to the moon," so I can anticipate the focus and tone of the speech.

A Closer Look

Although **"explain the benefits of such an endeavor"** didn't seem to tell me much about the text, the three aforementioned points reveal: (a) Kennedy's speech was likely aware of its audience and likely targeted those who would approve of his project (b) by giving them practical, as well as intangible, benefits, (c) all the while inspiring the nation by tapping into good-old-fashioned American patriotism.

So, I can safely assume the following things about the text:

1. **Tone:** the president's speech will carry rousing, "look over the horizon and imagine the possibilities" kind of tone.

2. **Target Audience:** the American people - the "look at all we've accomplished as a nation" American people.

3. **Speaker:** JFK will probably lean on the leadership of his ethos as the president of the United States, to "rally the troops."

4. **Subject:** the topic will concern the plan of sending an American to the moon. The main idea will likely be, "this may sound crazy, but we can do; look at everything else we've already done."

Prompt Analysis Questions

What is the speaker?
The speaker is more than the author, more than the person who's speaking, and more than the one who wrote the text. Who the speaker is helps you identify him: John F. Kennedy. What the speaker is lends life and personality to the speech, which will contribute to the analysis of the strategies he uses: the president of the United States - a man trying to convince a nation that it's time we went to the moon. Answering What the speaker is tells you about his/her ethos.

What is the situation?
The situation is more than contextualization. Context: yes, it's 1962, but what more? Situation: President Kennedy is young; is he trying to establish a legacy by taking us to the moon? Aren't we in the middle of a space race? Could he be responding to perceived threats to American safety? What is the situation? The situation can be derived from the text itself; meaning, the text will tell you what its context is and you have to make safe assumptions about the relationship of that context to the purpose of the text.

What is the audience?
This isn't given much attention because students assume that the audience is either the one mentioned in the prompt (the nondescript American populous) or you, who just happen to be reading the text at the moment, and therefore both perceptions offer little insight into the analysis of the text. Wrong. The question is "what values/morals/ideals/biases does the audience have?" And those values matter because they are the very ones the writer is usually appealing to in the text. The president speaking to the American people about going to the moon? Can you sense inspiration? Patriotism? We

can do it together! Yes. For JFK to succeed in this speech, he had to recognize his audience's wants and cater to them.

What is the point?

In a Rhetorical Analysis essay, the student writer must clearly **identify** the purpose of a text, as well as **evaluate its effectiveness.** The purpose of a text ranges from the **reason** for the writing (what set the author to compose the essay in the first place) to the **goal** of the writing (the agenda, the objective of the writer's argument).

Of course, the purpose of a text can vary; the writer may be trying to:
- arouse sympathy for a cause,
- incite outrage over an unjust circumstance,
- motivate the audience to take interest in something,
- prove/disprove an idea,
- support a cause or a person.

While the purpose is the most important part of the analysis, all of the other factors (speaker, audience, etc.) help to elucidate the purpose and offer evidence for it, so always **evaluate the purpose with at least two other factors in mind.** For example, in JFK's "To the Moon" speech, the prompt outlines the purpose as, "to explain the benefits of such an endeavor." So, the purpose is to sell America on going to the moon. Yes, the purpose has been identified.

Now, how successful is he? His speech has: inspirational moments, a hyperawareness of "falling behind" other countries, and a subtle handling of the money question. He has his audience in mind.

With all the different social and political problems plaguing 1960s America, how do you convince a country that we should go to the moon? Inspire. Unite. Make a patriotic call.

He is also aware of the occasion, the moment in history he inhabits. He relies on contemporary news about the space race and Russia's advancements, creating a sense of urgency (which is the tone), in his audience, and thus making his argument more appealing.

What is the subject?
The subject is tri-layered.

First, **the topic**. Using JFK's speech, the topic is space exploration compounded with human advancement.

Second, **the main idea**. Given the topic discussed, the main idea is progress, that because of our history of innovation, the next step for mankind is to be taken to the moon.

Third, **the theme**. The thematic concern of JFK's speech is not just about progress for progress' sake; at its core, this speech posits that we owe it to our humanity to dream and (quite literally) to reach for the stars.

READING THE TEXT

The last few sections have focused on the preliminary part of Rhetorical Analysis: **the prompt**. The sections covered: how to read it, understand it, and use it to the student's advantage when writing their response. Rhetorical Analysis must always begin with the prompt.

The next step, and the most complex and important step, is reading the text. It is complex because the student has to make so many different negotiations with the text in such a short amount of time:

    (1) what is happening?
    (2) to whom is the writer directing this?
    (3) what is the writer trying to accomplish?
    (4) what strategies is the writer using to accomplish the purpose?

But this step is the most important, because a poor reading of the text will result in a poor essay about the text, either because the students won't know enough about the text to be specific or because they will have completely misunderstood the text and have written about their misread instead. Both are bad.

There are **two steps**: the first tells the student what they should be looking for while they're reading the text, and the second tells them what they should be thinking about.

Step 1
I. Annotate
Annotations are a key component of any close reading and usually consist of a series of comments on the margins of the text or in a separate sheet of paper. Effective annotating is both economical and consistent. When annotating, students should keep in mind WHY they are annotating. "Can I use this in my essay?" That's the question to answer.

- Notice the persuasive appeals: **ethos, pathos, logos**.
- How is the text **organized**?
    o Problem at the beginning (or throughout), followed (sometimes ended) by a solution.
    o Cause of a circumstance or idea (usually a problem), followed by the effects it has had.
    o Whether the text is chronological or sequential.
    o Claim of something, followed by detailed evidence.

- Does the text offer a clear thesis or main idea (in order of occurrence: sometimes at the beginning of the text, sometimes at the end, and sometimes in the middle)?

II. List Devices
While reading the text, students will notice the different devices and strategies the writer is using. Some are obvious, like a metaphor or a simile, while some are subtle, like the sub-text of the author's criticism. The student must make several determinations about the devices.

Just because it's there, it doesn't mean it matters.
Sometimes a writer uses a metaphor in line 5, but it's only effective within a 3-sentence radius; it doesn't add or detract from the central focus of the text - that's a device. This metaphor is unlikely to prove too useful for meaningful conversation. There are times, however, when the writer uses

a metaphor to frame the entire issue of the text – that's a strategy. If so, students should consider it. The text will yield many devices, but students should concern themselves with the ones that are at the heart of the issue for a richer, more insightful essay.

Here are some (and I mean some) strategies to keep in mind:

- The way the author **selects evidence** to prove a point.

- The things that are **included and excluded** from the text.

- The **words** the writer uses, and the **connotations** they carry.

- The **images** the writer includes - are they thematic of the piece or only in certain portions of the text?

- The **appeal**(s) the writer prefers - does pathos work better for his audience?

- The **Figurative language** used: metaphor, simile, symbolism, analogy, allusion, etc.

- The way the writer addresses the **audience**.

- How is the **syntax** of the sentence? Long explicative sentences or short assertive sentences?

- How does the author manipulate **diction**? Repetition of certain words for a certain purpose.

- What **tone** does the text carry? Often, there will be a variety of tones used.

Step 2

Try to understand the text in sections, instead of lines. Maybe line 5 offers a metaphor that is interesting and appealing to the reader, but this device is only one of many that make the text rhetorically effective. Focus on **the effect an entire section has on the text** as a whole (say: the second paragraph, or the speaker's introductory remarks), and on how successful that section is in advancing the agenda of the text.

Excerpt from Kennedy's "To the Moon"

"No man can fully grasp how far and how fast we have come, but condense, if you will, the 50,000 years of man's recorded history in a time span of but a half-century. Stated in these terms, we know very little about the first 40 years, except at the end of them advanced man had learned to use the skins of animals to cover them. Then about 10 years ago, under this standard, man emerged from his caves to construct other kinds of shelter. Only five years ago man learned to write and use a cart with wheels. Christianity began less than two years ago. The printing press came this year, and then less than two months ago, during this whole 50-year span of human history, the steam engine provided a new source of power. Newton just explored the meaning of gravity. Last month electric lights and telephones and automobiles and airplanes became available. Only last week did we develop penicillin and television and nuclear power, and now if America's new spacecraft succeeds in reaching Venus, we will have literally reached the stars before midnight tonight."

Initial Analysis of the Excerpt

Early in his speech, Kennedy condenses the past "50,000 years of man's recorded history" into an allegorized 50 years, which gives human progress a fast pace, and in doing so, he lays the foundation for the sense of urgency his speech will have for going to the moon. Kennedy understands how preposterous it may seem to ask a nation to go to the moon, because the answer would be another question, "with what technology?" But his continued example, "...less than two months ago the steam engine provided a new source of power...[and] last month electric lights and telephones and automobiles and airplanes became available," sets his audience's gaze on possible technological horizons. After all, if the airplane just came last month, and "only last week did we develop penicillin and television and nuclear power," then it is definitely possible that "we will have literally reached the stars before midnight tonight." This re-understanding of history sets the mood for the rest of the speech by asking the audience to accept the possibility of leaving our planet, all the while inspiring them to do so.

Devices and Strategies

While reading the text, identify as many strategies as possible (how they work) and note their relationship to and impact on the text (why they work). Here is a comprehensive list of appeals and strategies you can identify while you read the text.

Appeals

a) **Ethos** – credibility. Do I **trust**/relate to the writer? Consider the author's credentials, as mentioned in the prompt – is he/she **competent**? Consider the language the writer uses in the text to ascertain knowledge, experience, likeability and personality. Are they **reliable**?

b) **Pathos** – emotional. What does the text want me to feel? Consider the language: Loaded? Manipulative? Vivid? Humorous? What effect does it have on the intended audience? The key is not to think about the emotional response you're having to the text, but to **consider the emotional response the writer is trying to make his audience have.**

c) **Logos** – logic. What does the writer want me to think? Consider the **facts**, definitions, quotations, informed opinions and examples used. On what **evidence** is the writer basing his argument? Is his evidence **sensible**?

Style

a) **Diction**

- Pay attention to the type of words the writer uses and the connotations they carry. Are the words formal or conversational? Consider **Word Choice**.

- Consider if there any **shifts** in language - the writer can show restraint at the beginning and become more indignant, as the text continues.

- What attitude (tone) do the words reveal?

- Are the verbs aggressive? Are the adjectives thematically related?

- When talking about diction, try not to fixate on a word or two; rather, show the **interrelatedness** of the words throughout the text.

Example

"The writer repeats the word "we" throughout his article, in order to establish collective blame for the black communities' lack of political involvement and emphasize the importance of unity in securing colored's rights. In fact, he begins his article with this word, stating that "we (blacks) need an organ for making our voice heard" (1-2). By using "we," he collectively blames freedmen's lack of participation in activism, for the black community's misrepresentation in media."

b) **Syntax**

- How are the sentences constructed? **Simple sentences** are usually shorter and they contain the writer's claims, while **complex sentences** are usually lengthy and they concern themselves with explaining the writer's claim.

- Are there thoughts **repeated** in the same paragraph, though not verbatim? Does this create emphasis/importance? Do the sentences add up to a big idea?

- Are there any **questions** in the text? What do they imply?

- Syntax often yields little insight in student essays, when presented in isolation; however, if you can **tie the syntactical observation to a theme,** you'll have a better analysis.

Example
"when discussing the experience of poverty, the writer elongates one sentence to the size of a paragraph in order to exemplify the poor man's destitution and dramatize the never-ending feeling poverty can have on a person's psyche."

   c) **Figurative Language**

      - Are there images or repetitions of imagery in the text?

      - Are there metaphors, similes, analogies, hyperboles, anaphora, understatements, personifications, irony, or allegories?

      - These are so common in an R.A. text that students frequently mention them. The problem is when the student makes no connection between the figurative language and the purpose of the text.

Bad Example
"Abigail Adams uses a simile when she compares her son's journey to Paris to a river "growing away" from its source."
So what?

Better Example
"When Abigail Adams compares her son's journey to Paris to a river "growing away" from its source, she implies that both will grow stronger as they journey away from home." Say more.

Best Example
"Abigail Adams compares her son's journey to Paris to a river growing into the sea, because they both leave their little streams of knowledge and influence, into an ocean of opportunity – an apt simile, considering that her son

would've spent the past months on a ship and this comparison would be more personal to him."

d) Tone

- What is the **attitude of the text**? Pay attention to the adjectives and verbs; they can reveal the writer's approach to the issue. In the case of satire, be mindful of hyperboles and understatements.

- There is usually more than one attitude, or rather, attitudes **(tones) can shift** throughout the text. Consider the key words that may signal these changes (the usual suspects: but, however, etc.). These shifts can be very subtle too, so look for the omitted word that reveals negation or contradiction.

- Tone is notoriously **elusive** because it can be stated directly or indirectly, but the key is to consider the context, as a means to inferring what the words may be implying.

<u>Example:</u>
"The reader can assume a certain degree of maternal concern (tone) from Abigail Adams' letter to her traveling son, but verify that assumption with her choice of words. In her letter, that maternal tone manifests as stern admonition of her son's expressed desires to return home, and can at times, seem like scolding. So, a complete understanding of the letter's tone, would have to acknowledge that admonition and include that it stems from a mother's love, because she wants her son to take advantage of the opportunity to be living in France, as a young American."

Devices vs. Strategies

The difference between "device" and "strategy" is subtle enough that it is important to note. For the sake of this guide and for my own classroom instruction, I teach devices and strategies in the following way.

A **device** is a tool the writer uses to strengthen the argument of the text. Devices are easily recognized in terms like: metaphor, anaphora, simile, etc. These tools are usually of a single-purpose use and do not always apply to the complete work.

While devices are tools the writer uses to enhance the writing, **strategies** are the methods the writer uses to accomplish an intended purpose. Also understood as an approach, a strategy offers an extended understanding of the device, often including another, that provides the context in which the device functions. Essentially, a device is a thing; a strategy is what it does.

Example
In a letter to her son, Abigail Adams creates a simile between her son and a river, in order to encourage him in his travels away from home:

> "as a river increases in strength the farther the stream travels from the source, so shall you..." This **simile is a device.**

The **strategy** is the next step – explaining how the writer uses that device (and perhaps other devices) to appeal to the reader in a certain way.

Here's the difference
The following three examples demonstrate how a student-writer can turn a device into a strategy that can exemplify the stated purpose of the Rhetorical Analysis text.

Identifying the device and how it works

Abigail Adams uses a simile in order to compare her son's journey away from home to that of a river flowing away from a stream.

Making the device into a strategy

Abigail Adams compares her son's journey across the ocean to that of a river's, increasing in strength and wisdom, as they both travel away from home.

Making two devices into a strategy

Abigail Adams compares her son's journey across the ocean to that of a river's, increasing in strength and wisdom, as they both travel away from home. She compounds her simile with allusions to the other great men, who like her son, traveled far from home and made a name for themselves in the process, to encourage her son to see this trip as an opportunity and not an imposition.

WRITING THE ESSAY

INTRODUCTION

Introductions are best when they are succinct. Too short and it will seem rushed. Too lengthy and it will seem as if you're beginning a discussion that is best saved for the body paragraphs. For a good first impression, write about 2-3 sentences.

Quick Intro Tips

- **Don't** make it too lengthy. You don't have the time, and neither does the reader.

- **Don't** talk about your personal experiences.

- **Do** identify the Rhetorical **Device** and explain its effect on the text. Rhetorical Devices should be explained in the context of a larger strategy.

- **Don't** define Rhetorical Devices. For instance, don't write, "the writer uses a simile to compare A to B." That's what similes do; they compare. Instead, say, "the writer compares Adams' journey to Europe to that of a river because _____."

- **Do** offer insight into the **purpose of the writing**. Misidentifying the purpose of the writing, will not score you more than a 4.

- **Do** identify the **tone** of the writing by using adjectives or verbs that are familiar to those of the text.

1st Sentence — Setting the Stage
(Topic/Theme, Speaker and Subject)

Some writers begin with a **metaphor** that relates to the theme or a **quotation** from the text, or with some **personal insight** they've gathered from their reading. These are fine. I recommend beginning with a compound sentence that has two specific parts:

> **1.** The first part should be something **topical** (sometimes thematic).
> **2.** the second part should introduce the **speaker**, **subject**, and (if needed), the **audience**.

Example
To writers like Leonid Fridman, American society has historically adopted a scorning and ostracizing attitude towards the academically-gifted individuals who form the intelligentsia of society.

Rationale
Deferring to the writer of the text, allows the student-writer to use the phrase "historically adopted…" without having to provide examples to substantiate. The context of society's "scorning and ostracizing attitude toward the academically-gifted" sets the precedent for a (later) connection to the writer's purpose. What's more, the comment of "individuals who form the intelligentsia of society…" focuses the conversation on what the text later refers to as "nerds and geeks," and provides better language than the aforementioned derogatory terms.

2nd Sentence — Context
(Speaker, Situation and Audience)

The second sentence is about **context**. The idea is to frame the conversation.

Keep in mind:

1. Writer: if you haven't already, introduce the writer of the text you're analyzing. If you have, introduce something new about the writer, other than he's a writer. Introducing something new about the writer (like: he's a lawyer, or she's a doctor) will afford you greater opportunities for deeper analysis.

2. Audience: the writer of the text is never addressing a mass of faceless people called, "the audience." There's always an intended audience - a certain kind of people. The faster you identify who and what they are, the more comprehensive your analysis will be.

Example

In his essay, "America needs its nerds," an **indignant** Fridman **decries** that there is a fundamental issue in how **Americans view intellectuals** and promotes a shift in attitude towards cultural perception and treatment of academics.

Rationale

The student writer identifies Fridman as "indignant" and uses the verb "decries" to emphasize the tone, and the audience's perception of intelligence as having "a fundamental issue." The latter part of the essay introduces the purpose of the text, "promotes a shift in attitude towards cultural perception and treatment of academics." This allows the student-writer to dedicate more time to the explanation in the next sentences.

3rd Sentence   **Thesis**
(Purpose of text, Rhetorical Strategies, Rhetorical Devices + Tone)

This sentence is tricky. It doesn't have to be the third sentence, but it should be the last. Definitely no more than that. This sentence should directly address the task of the prompt without directly quoting from the prompt.

The task is always, "What strategies does _____ use to accomplish _____." It is in responding to this task that you formulate your thesis.

Things you need in a <u>thesis</u>:

   - Writer's **name** (or pronoun)

   - **Purpose** (or aim) of the writing. This is your **claim**.

   - STRONG **verb** that clarifies the impact and function of the rhetorical devices.

   - **Rhetorical Devices**, to be discussed in the body paragraphs. These are your **reasons**.

   - **Rhetorical Strategies**, which give shape to the devices and demonstrate that you understand the situation surrounding the devices.

   - Specific **adjectives** throughout this sentence can offer insight about the tone of the text, to your reader.

Parts of the Thesis

There are three components of the thesis that demand scrutiny: <u>Claim, Evidence, and Rationale</u>.

These components can be expressed in three different ways: *What, How, Why*. These are the crucial elements of a thesis statement, in most essays, and especially in Rhetorical Analysis.

WHAT
This is the **claim** of your essay. The claim is your assertion of something. In the case of Rhetorical Analysis, your assertion concerns **the purpose of the text**. Essentially, the claim of your essay states what you understand is the claim and intention of the text you read. If you think the text seeks to convince the reader of the value of something, then that's your claim. Hence, misunderstanding the text will result in an invalid claim.

HOW
This is the **evidence** that supports your claim, sometimes called the reasons. In Rhetorical Analysis, these reasons concern the **devices** used by the author to accomplish his purpose.

WHY
This is the **rationale** of the evidence provided, and how it contributes to the author's message. In Rhetorical Analysis, this relates to the **strategies** used by the author to reach his underlying meaning. This rationale should go beyond the text.

Thesis Example

He does so by appealing to national pride through comparisons between America and East Asia and by using micro-examples to exemplify the irony of how intellectuals are viewed. In doing so, he creates a cohesive argument that condemns American attitude towards intellectuals and promotes intellectualism.

Rationale

WHAT

The phrase, "he does so" relies on the noun phrase from the previous sentence, where the student-writer establishes the purpose. Doing this, gives the writer two advantages:

    1. the sentence is smaller (because it replaces the claim with "he does so") and therefore much more focused on the devices and strategies.

    2. The student-writer can now end the introduction with a reiteration of the claim (because it only previously used "he does so"), and ending with this declarative sentence makes for an emphatic last sentence.

HOW

The first device of the thesis, "...by appealing to national pride" is explained with the use of "comparisons between..." but the second device, "... using micro-examples" begs the question: what micro-examples? Perhaps if the sentence read, "...using micro-examples" of this or that, the point would be a little bit stronger.

WHY

The rationales, which are the strategies, further explain the two devices aforementioned: "...through comparisons between America and East Asia" "...to exemplify the irony of how intellectuals are viewed"

Complete Introduction Example

(1) To writers like Leonid Fridman, American society has historically adopted a scorning and ostracizing attitude towards the academically-gifted individuals who form the intelligentsia of society. (2) In his essay, "America needs its nerds," an indignant Fridman decries that there is a fundamental issue in how Americans view intellectuals and promotes a shift in attitude towards cultural perception and treatment of academics. (3) He does so by appealing to national pride through comparisons between America and East Asia and by using micro-examples to exemplify the irony of how intellectuals are viewed. (4) In doing so, he creates a cohesive argument that condemns American attitude towards intellectuals and promotes intellectualism.

More Examples of Introductions

Introduction A: As the saying goes, mother knows best. In Abigail Adams' letter to her son John Quincy Adams, she proudly offers her advice to her reluctant son on the advantages of his travels abroad. Adams tackles her son's disinclination towards being away from home, through the use of a maternal, emotional connection and sagacious comparisons. **(Score 5).**

> **Rationale for the score:** the first two sentences frame the conversation adequately, but the last sentence (the thesis sentence) lacks an understanding of the author's strategy. The sentence recognizes the purpose, "Adams tackles her son's disinclination..." and the devices, "maternal, emotional...comparisons" but it does not clarify the strategy surrounding the device. Maternal connection that does what? Sagacious comparisons that do what?

Introduction B: It is held by all Americans that all men are created equal and freedom must be fought for and protected. Alfred Green's speech in 1861 advocates these principles by urging his African American audience to campaign for the right to participate in the Civil War. Green constantly refines his argument and confronts the counter arguments, in order to ignite a determination in his audience to earn the ability to fight for the equality granted to all men and to abolish the "tyrant system of slavery." **(Score 6, 7).**

> **Rationale for the score:** the introduction begins with an attempt to give historical context, although no real information is provided, just a blanket statement, "It is held by...protected." With this considered, the introduction is still effective because of a strong thesis which offers insight into the author's purpose: "Green constantly refines...determination."

Introduction C: The American dream has always been to expand horizons and search for new frontiers – a concept that Edmund Bell would agree with due to his own experiences with migration. His belief that migrating to new locations is "inherently good," is refuted in Evan Starr's article, "Leaving a Life for Another." Edmund is meticulous as he reveals that establishing permanent residence is of value due to the respect gained for the environment once it is settled in. He convinces supporters of constant movement that migration does always provide beneficial results through the recurrence of a migrational theme and direct acknowledgement of the opposition. **(Score 7).**

Rationale for the score: successful contextualization is accomplished with a solid first sentence that flows well and gives necessary information. The student then provides effective insight into Bell's reasoning: "'is meticulous as he...settled in." He further develops his thesis by explaining Bell's strategies: "migrational theme and direct acknowledgement of the opposition." What makes this introduction most effective is the student-writer's display of a thorough understanding of the text.

BODY

The body paragraph constitutes the bulk of your essay and it is the most important part of the writing. An effective (R.A.) body paragraph analyzes the strategies found in the text, in order to determine if the writer was successful in accomplishing his/her purpose.

The analysis can be done
    chronologically (going through the strategies at the beginning, middle, and end of the text) or
    sectionally (focusing on the prominent strategies in the first section of the text, and then the second – it may vary depending on the organization of the text).

For an effective body paragraph, no less than 5 and no more than 10 sentences are recommended.

Quick Body Tips

- **Tie the analysis to a specific portion of text.** You don't always have to say that your analysis concerns lines 5 and 6, but mention that your point relates to "the first paragraph," or "the first half of the text" or "near the end of the passage."

- **Connect every point to the purpose of the text.** The first part is to identify the strategies and the second (and most important) part is to explain how those strategies help the text achieve its purpose.

- Not everything in the text matters. **Be selective.**

1st Sentence	WHAT
Claim (Strategy + Rationale)	

The body paragraph begins with a **topical sentence** that determines the direction of that paragraph. This sentence includes one of the **strategies** mentioned in the thesis and its **rationale**. Essentially, this sentence answers WHAT this body paragraph will be about.

Example
Understanding that **his audience may not recognize** or have an invested interest in decrying America's anti-intellectualism, Fridman **compares the treatment of scholars** in the U.S. and East Asia, to **appeal** to American's national pride and stimulate competitive improvement.

Rationale
The student-writer **identifies the audience** of the original work as people who "may not recognize or have an invested interest in decrying America's anti-intellectualism." In doing so, the strategy that follows, "appeal to American's national pride," is **contextualized and substantiated by the device**, "compares the treatment of scholars in the U.S. and East Asia." This adds to the overall **purpose** of this section of passage, which is to "stimulate competitive improvement," by encouraging intellectualism.

2nd Sentence (as many as you need)   HOW
Support, Evidence, Reasons, Examples

The next part of the body paragraph discusses the effects the strategy has on the text. These sentences explain the first sentence by detailing HOW the claim makes sense; this can be done through the use of quotations, explanations, examples, elaboration on those examples and further commentary of the strategy covered in this body.

Recommendations

- Focus your conversation on **one strategy**, even if it includes several devices.

- Explain how the **strategy helps the text accomplish its purpose** ("by using this, the writer accomplishes that"), using important portions from the text.

- **Quote** a small portion of the text (no more than a line and a half), being careful to cite the line number afterwards (5).

- Follow or precede each quotation with some form of **commentary** on the quotation introduced. This commentary may serve as your initial analysis of the quotation or as explanation to the reader of the context around the quotation.

- Beyond the commentary, offer insight by **connecting one quotation** to some other quotation (or paraphrase) from the text, all relating to the same strategy.

Example

This is evident in the latter part of his essay, when he states that in industrialized East Asian nations, "a kid who studies hard is **lauded** and held up **as an example** to other students" (39) while a kid who is studious in America is ostracized and "**haunted to the grave**" (32). One would imagine that the more intellectuals in a region, the more likely the area **benefits from the innovation and knowledge generated by them**; so, when Fridman states that there are unencouraging disparities in American treatment of intellectuals when compared to East Asia, he implies that the **ostracization of academics has resulted in a scarcity of them** and the innovative knowledge they offer. Innovation fuels development and with less academics in America than in East Asia, Fridman suggests that, eventually, devaluing of intellectuals in the U.S. is going to result in a **shortage of scholars and therefore a lag in our development**. Even though our culture does not regard individuals who study hard and pursue academia, it does value the pursuit of excellence and the idea that the U.S. is the best in the world. While Americans might not want to alter their treatment of intellectuals for their own sake they would do so for the benefit of their country.

Rationale

The use of examples like, "lauded and held up as an example," and "haunted to the grave," provide sufficient contrast between the U.S. and East Asian nations, which signals to the conversation of patriotism, established in the last sentence. Then, by suggesting, "one would imagine that the more intellectuals in a region, the more likely the area benefits from the innovation and knowledge generated by them," the student-writer's extends the conversation to national competition, which connects to the text's implication, "that the ostracization of academics has resulted in a scarcity of them, and the innovative knowledge they offer." This idea is capitalized in the following sentence, where the student-writer makes explicit, that "devaluing of intellectuals in the U.S. is going to result in a shortage of scholars and therefore a lag in our development." The student-writer then assumes, as Fridman also assumes, a sense of complacency from his audience, by stating, "even though our culture does not regard individuals who study hard and pursue academia," which is then connected to the overall claim of the body paragraph (patriotism and national competition) by adding, "it does value the pursuit of excellence and the idea that the U.S. is the best in the world." With this, the student-writer extends Fridman's argument that, "Americans might not want to alter their treatment of intellectuals for their own sake they would do so for the benefit of their country."

Last Sentence	WHY
Offer Insight	

This last sentence **reflects on what has been discussed** throughout the body paragraph. This sentence doesn't make any claims or offer any explanations because they've already been provided; this sentence should signal to the reader the conclusion your paragraph has arrived to.

Example
With this **sobering** realization, **steeped in nationalistic pride**, Fridman creates an effective call to action that demands a new outlook on intellectualism.

Rationale
The insight provided in this last sentence names "Fridman's call to action," a "sobering realization, steeped in nationalistic pride," which further reiterates the text's purpose and hope, for "a new outlook on intellectualism."

Complete Body Paragraph Example

Understanding that his audience may not feel motivated to take action against America's anti-intellectualism, Fridman compares the treatment of scholars in the U.S. and East Asia, to appeal to American's national pride and stimulate competitive improvement. This is evident in the latter part of his essay, when he states that in industrialized East Asian nations, "a kid who studies hard is lauded and held up as an example to other students" [Line 39] while a kid who is studious in America is ostracized and "haunted to the grave" [32]. One would imagine that the more intellectuals in a region, the more likely the area benefits from the innovation and knowledge generated by them; so, when Fridman states that there are unencouraging disparities in American treatment of intellectuals when compared to East Asia, he implies that the ostracization of academics has resulted in a scarcity of them and the innovative knowledge they offer. Innovation fuels development and with less academics in America than in East Asia, Fridman suggests that, eventually, devaluing of intellectuals in the U.S. is going to result in a shortage of scholars and therefore a lag in our development. Even though our culture does not regard individuals who study hard and pursue academia, it does value the pursuit of excellence and the idea that the U.S. is the best in the world. While Americans might not want to alter their treatment of intellectuals for their own sake they would do so for the benefit of their country. With this sobering realization, steeped in nationalistic pride, Fridman creates an effective call to action that demands a new outlook on intellectualism.

More Examples of Body Paragraphs

Body A: Adams is insistent as she enlightens her son on the worth of his travels by eliciting a parental emotional connection. She hints that her son's future success will be due to the advantageous opportunities granted to him, "under the instructive eye of a tender parent," (lines 22-23) and thus reveals that it is unacceptable for him to fail at acquiring intellectuality through his experiences abroad. Adams goes further by annunciating, "render your parents supremely happy, particularly, your ever-affectionate mother," (lines 61-63) to attack any opposition against her counseling, while simultaneously annunciating her the disappointment that will ensue if he resists. **(Score 6)**

Rationale for the score: "is insistent as she enlightens" is an awkward phrase, as well as, "on the worth of his travels." However, the sentence does establish Adams' use of a "parental emotional connection" as the guiding direction of the body discussion, which makes the paragraph focused. The body paragraph blends quotations well and provides adequate insight, like: "thus reveals that it is unacceptable..." It is adequate only because it is surface insight.

Body B: Abigail Adams, through the use of sensible comparisons, teaches her son the values of the experiences he will face in his travels away from home. She strives towards demonstrating the advantages of his education when she alludes to an author who, "compares a judicious traveler to a river," because just as the river continues to enhance its qualities as it surges, so will the knowledge he obtains by willingly participating in the experiences he encounters on his travels away from home (lines 16-20). Adams also describes wisdom and "penetration" as the "fruit of experience" (lines 35-36) to signify that there is value in exposure to opportunities, in order to convince her son that he will gain significant virtues if he is open to the experience. **(Score 6, 7)**

Rationale for the score: notwithstanding phrases like "she strives *towards* demonstrating" and "there is value in *exposure to opportunities*," which are awkward, the body paragraph provides more than adequate analysis of the purpose of the text, as well as more than sufficient insight on quotations. For instance, when quoting Adams' simile where she compares a judicious traveler to a river, the student writer adds, "because just as the river continues to enhance its qualities as it surges, so will the knowledge he obtains by willingly participating in the experiences he encounters on his travels away from home." This addition provides more than simple commentary on the text and ties into the overall purpose.

Body C: Thoreau tackles the significance of autonomy against an inhibiting government, by advocating his values on transcendentalism to inspire changes in his audience. He says, "I could not help being struck with foolishness of that institution which treated me as if I were mere flesh and blood and bones to be locked up," (paragraph 26) in order to emphasize that his soul is of more value than his body, which in turn taints the inexpedient government's reputation and establishes Thoreau's credibility. He also highlights how people are not the government's "means to an end" and how they view citizens as "machines with bodies" that they can use for their own will, when they should be treated as individuals that do not just have bodies but consciences (paragraph 5). Thoreau evokes the audience's support for his argument by showing his concern for the unmerited treatment of the populace. **(Could be a 9)**

Rationale for the score: the body is consistent in its use of elevated language, blends quotations well, offers keen insight not readily apparent in an initial reading of the text, and uses verbs evocatively all throughout. What I like most about this body, and what I consider to be the most important aspect of a body paragraph, is the ability to quote the text, explain the quote and then explain your explanation; this is true insight.

CONCLUSION

- Be **brief**. No more than 3 sentences.

- Do NOT summarize everything you've said.

- No new quotations or comments on the text. You've said everything you needed to say in the body paragraph.

- Do not restate the strategies; instead, talk about their combined effect on the text.

Examples

One Sentence Conclusion
Samuel Johnson reasonably denies this woman's request to give her son a letter of recommendation because he does not know him well enough to do so, and ends his letter with a sensible explanation along with a compliment to her child, leaving both parties feeling satisfied and guilt-free.
(Score 5, 6)

By questioning American antagonism of intellectuals, Friedman seeks to change these long-standing views and implement superior ones in their place arguing that by ostracizing the intellectually inclined and academically motivated, Americas is only ostracizing itself from a more tolerant and accepting world. **(Score 8, 9)**

Two-Sentence Conclusion
Forlorn and forgotten are the men who truly rode the wave of their countries, their hearts not wise enough to Bell constructs his perception of migration by effectively playing off Starr's beliefs and through the repetition of themes relating to movement. He is calculating, yet respectful as he builds his argument and demonstrates that by becoming inhabitants rather than visitors, people can finally make a home for themselves and future generations. **(Score 9)**

Bell constructs his perception of migration by effectively playing off Starr's beliefs and through the repetition of themes relating to movement. He is calculating, yet respectful as he builds his argument and demonstrates that by becoming inhabitants rather than visitors, people can finally make a home for themselves and future generations. **(Score 5, 6)**

Three-Sentence Conclusions
In the end, all of these scenes can only be valuable if people stop to acknowledge and admire them. Louv advocates the separation of man and nature by using descriptive language and an example of human interference to promote nature as a being worthy of value and preservation. Although it is human nature to have as much control as possible, not everything in life needs to be controlled. **(Score 5)**

PACING THE ESSAY
(40 mins.)

What follows is a recommended timetable for the composition of the Rhetorical Analysis essay, within the allotted time of 40 minutes. While the timing and process of composition will vary from writer to writer, the breakdown below offers a realistic and effective approach to use the day of the test.

10 minutes

(The Prompt)
 1. Read the question carefully. **Read it again**. Don't read the text yet.
 2. Pay close attention to **the purpose and strategies** (a hint of the purpose can be found at the end of the prompt).
 3. **Before writing anything**, be sure you understand what is being asked.

(The Text)
 1. Read the text. Either: (1) **read it through twice** at a brisk pace or (2) **read it once slowly** and carefully. It depends on the kind of text you get and your preference.
 2. As you read through the text, **identify** (circle, underline) **rhetorical devices**, organizational patterns, word choices, or anything else you can use in your own writing.

(The Thesis)
 1. **Draft an initial thesis** BEFORE beginning your essay. It doesn't have to be too sophisticated. You'll have time for that later. Simply, draft something simple, such as: Abigail Adams (Purpose + Verb) by (Rhetorical Strategy).
 2. If you have the time, **lay out a tentative organization for your body paragraphs**: first, you'll

talk about this, and then you'll talk about that. Simple. Don't over-plan. You'll plan later.

25 minutes

(The essay)
1. **Plan your essay!**
2. Write about **two or three important strategies and devices**, and how they help the writer accomplish his/her purpose. **Don't write** about **every device** you notice. If you do, it will feel rushed.
3. **Connect every paragraph.** Readers don't like it when you jump from one idea to another without a proper bridge. The best way to be organized is to keep the prompt in mind.
4. Try to **write 2 full pages.** A moderate intro (no more than 4 sentences), two hearty body paragraphs (7-10 sentences) and a modest conclusion (2-3 sentences) should do the job.

5 minutes

(The revision)
1. Proofread your essay, looking for misspelled words or punctuation errors. You don't have time to redo an entire section in the last 5 minutes. **Worry about the simple things you can fix**, like rewriting an illegible word or crossing out the extra "the."

Complete Rhetorical Analysis Essay Examples

This section includes a selection of Rhetorical Analysis essays; each scored, like many of the paragraphs presented beforehand, ranging from mid to high. I decided not to include low-scoring essays because their glaring issues often make them easier to recognize. So I included essays that are neither all good nor all bad, instead, they are - each of them - good and bad, with laudable moments and page-tearing-what-were-you-thinking moments; not only does this varying quality makes them more challenging to score, but realistically, that is how essays are written, with good, bad, and ugly moments.

Essay #1

There are certain arguments that seem impossible to make, because the answer seems so clear, it is hard to imagine an argument at all; such is the argument of slavery. While today, slavery is obviously illegal and immoral, in 1791, when Benjamin Banneker – a slave's son – wrote to Thomas Jefferson on the issue, slavery was a point of political contention, not morality. In his letter, Banneker introduces the modern, moral argument to slavery, asking Jefferson to do his part in ending the extensive suffering and cruelty slaves face. Banneker also draws a parallel between Jefferson's beliefs enumerated by the Declaration of Independence and the plight of slaves, showing the logical progression in that, if it is the new nation's right to liberty, then surely it is the slave's right as well.

One of slavery's early opponents was Benjamin Banneker, who in 1791 implored Jefferson to "wean [the nation] from those narrow prejudices [of slavery]" (line 46-47). In his comparison of the slaves to Job (line 48-50), Banneker makes the argument against slavery wholly moral by introducing a religious precedent for his position, indicating that the nation should not "counteract [God's] mercies" (line 36) with "fraud and violence so numerous…groaning captivity and cruel oppression" (37-39). While the moral argument is strong, Banneker needs Jefferson's political sway to have anything accomplished. By indicting Jefferson himself, claiming he has been "found guilty of that most criminal act [slavery] which you professedly detested" (line 39-41), showing that politics can sway a man to slavery, indicating that they may also be used to sway a man from slavery, and urging Jefferson to stick with his original morals.

Other than a moral argument, Banneker presents Jefferson with a logical one. If the American people can claim freedom from the "tyranny of the British Crown" (line 2), then surely slaves should claim freedom as well. He used Jefferson's own words against him, "We hold these truths to be self-evident, that all men are created equal, and are endowed…with certain inalienable rights…life, liberty, and the pursuit of happiness" (line 21-25). Jefferson himself enumerated the right of all to freedom, of the "valuation of liberty and the free possession of those blessings to which you were entitled by nature" (line 29-30). Which then begs the questions of why a nation founded on liberty, would withhold "impartial distribution of those rights and privileges" (line 33-34) from all its inhabitants. It stands to reason then, that if Americans had a right to freedom, so did American slaves. Banneker draws the parallel between the plight of the slaves, and that of the American Revolution in such a way that that Jefferson, and by extension American politicians, would have no other conclusion to draw. Banneker even ends his letters, "thus shall [Jefferson] need neither the direction of myself or others, in what manner to proceed herein" (line 51-53), he is so confident in his argument, he doesn't feel the need to spell out that he wants Jefferson to curb slavery as he works on building the new nation. Jefferson was building the nation on the premise of freedom, but Banneker was pointing out that he was building the nation on hypocrisy.

Slavery is a moral wrong in the modern day, but for the first century of America's history, it was a political right. So contentious was the issue, it lead to the civil war, which many believe could have been avoided if the founders had curbed slavery from the start. When the nation was in its infancy, a son of slaves wrote to Thomas Jefferson, a man who wrote of inalienable rights, and in drawing parallels between Jefferson and himself and in making a moral argument, asked the same for his people, because if America was truly to be a land of the free, then how could so many continue to be oppressed?

(Score 7, 8)

Essay #2

The Onion is a satirical publication that tackles popular subjects in today's media and spins them into a mockery of themselves. In 1999, the magazine took on consumerism and marketing in the modern age, in the form of an insole infomercial. By employing a simulacrum of medical jargon and numerous logical fallacies, the author shows the fallaciousness of advertisements and the gullibility of consumers.

By sounding like an infomercial, the article becomes one; it has all of the diction of one but, by adding pseudoscientific details, shows the ridiculousness of retail. The author employs the stereotypical buzzwords of an advertisement, such as "clamoring," "exciting," and "effective," all to entice the customer into buying a product. In this editorial, the author takes that principle and blows it out of proportion. The author interjects words such as "pseudoscience," "bio-flow," and "semi-plausible" all to show the implausibility of the commercial. Then, the writer takes it a step further and speaks of fake medicinal practices, such as reflexology, the "correspondence between every point on the human foot and another part of the body" (Line 23) and terranometry, which "converts the wearer's own energy to match the Earth's natural vibrational rate" (Line 46). These distorted medicinal practices parody real life marketing strategies, which use scientific-sounding words to lure the consumers into a false sense of trust in order to sell them a product. By employing the stereotypical syntax and diction of a commercial, The Onion satirizes the American consumerist ideals.

The article utilizes a number of logical fallacies, such as slippery slope, appeal to authority, and trust in peers, all to appeal to the consumer's psyche to make them buy the product. The logical fallacy of a slippery slope is in which a series of very small steps results in a huge effect; usually, the events do not correlate, as in the article. Whenever the author employs pseudoscientific aspects in the product, a slippery slope defines how the particular method works, as in terranometry, which establishes the fact "the Earth resonates on very precise frequency" (Line 39) and then snowballs out of proportion to say "if the frequency of one's foots is out of alignment with the Earth, the entire body will suffer" (Line 43). The slippery slope follows a very weak logic in order to push its own agenda towards the customer and instill a false sense of trust. Another logical fallacy employed is the appeal to authority. Throughout the article, "pseudoscientists" advertise the insoles, and herald their healing properties. The article itself calls the practice out, stating "I can pay twenty dollars for insoles clearly endorsed by an intelligent-looking man in a white lab coat" (Line 67). People trust authority figures, such as scientists, and will buy a product if advertised by such. The Onion also uses trust in peers to sell MagnaSoles. At the end of the piece, there are customer reviews, raving about the quality of the insoles when, in reality, the product did not help their situation. Customer Helene Kuhn twisted her ankle seven weeks prior to buying MagnaSoles and noticed "a significant decrease in pain and can now walk comfortably" (Line 56). In reality, the insoles did not cure her ankle, seven weeks of healing did. But, commercials expect consumers to listen to these satisfied customers and take their word for it and buy the product. By satirizing the gullibility of consumerist, the article shows the ridiculousness of modern day commercials.

Utilizing the diction and logical fallacies of advertisements, The Onion parodies and shows the innate flaws in today's consumerist society, where people are easily swayed into buying meaningless and useless products.

(Score 8)

Essay #3

American society has become increasingly plagued by mindless consumerism, centered on the purchase of well-advertised, needless products. The Onion, a publication devoted to humor and satire, ridicules this phenomenon in their piece on how products are marketed to consumers. By employing pseudoscientific diction, where the words used belie their authenticity, in addition to incorporating logical fallacies that appeal to a false authority and lead the reader down a slippery slope, they accomplish a cohesive, satirical argument that emphasizes the idiocy of modern consumerism.

In order to make obvious the satirical nature of their article, The Onion repeats the word pseudoscience throughout the text and employs pseudoscientific "data" to falsely advertise the MagnaSoles. For example, in line 5 the author writes that the MagnaSole shoe insert "stimulates and soothes the wearer's feet using no fewer than five forms of pseudoscience." Given that the word pseudoscience is mentioned directly at the beginning of the article to describe how the insoles work, this stresses to the reader that the basis of the information is fake. However, the purpose of The Onion in writing this piece is to prove to readers how they may know advertising information is fake, yet they still believe it and end up buying faulty products. Therefore, in paragraph 6 the writer goes on to mention how the insoles are able to conduct their purpose by "matching one's own energy with that of the Earth's own vibrational rate at 32.085 kilofrankels." The information provided in this line may sound scientific, but at closer inspection it is completely contrived: a kilofrankel is not a real scientific measurement and there is no known relationship between an individual's energy and that of the Earth. To the careless consumer, however this may sound like legitimate information and they may buy the product without thinking twice. By employing this strategy, the writer emphasizes how believing individuals are and how easily they succumb to the charm of information that is at close inspection entirely fictitious.

Understanding how modern advertising functions, the author of the article includes logical fallacies that appeal to a false authority and lead the reader down a slippery slope, to simulate latent advertising techniques. This is evident throughout the article, when the author states that according to Dr. Wayne Frankel, the Californian State University "biotrician who discovered Terranometry, MagnaSoles soothe the feet by aligning the frequency of one's foot with the Earth." Given that consumers are quick to believe anything that comes out the mouth of a "liscensed professional," especially one with educational expertise, individuals who hear this "evidence" probably ignore the fact that the information cited, makes no logical nor scientific sense. The Onion also includes a slippery slope logical fallacy in their publication, when they state that "if the frequency of one's foot is out of alignment with the Earth, the entire body will suffer" (Line 45). By asserting that positioning is a direct cause of suffering, the writer creates a frightful, yet totally false statement that may scare a consumer into buying the product without once considering the fact that there is no known relationship between these two factors. In combination, these two logical fallacies exemplify the tricks employed by modern advertising and emphasize the lack of caution exercised by consumers.

Essentially, The Onion employs pseudoscientific diction and logical fallacies to create a satirical wake-up-call for individuals who purchase needless, faulty goods. In doing so, they highlight the detriments that are associated with the mindlessness and superficiality of a culture centered on consumerism.

(Score 7)

The Almost Adequate Essay

One of the most difficult essays, and one of my most commonly scored essays, is the **5/6 essay**. This is the essay that stands in the threshold of inadequate (4) and could've entered into adequate (6), but it isn't bad enough to be the former nor good enough to be the latter. These can be a challenge. The key is to remember what adequate essays read like:

6 Adequate

These essays **get the job done**: presenting a **clear thesis**, though **not** particularly **sophisticated**, and organizing **focused ideas** in developed paragraphs. However, they may offer sufficiently developed textual examples, with less detailed and/or **less convincing superficial explanations**. These essays provide more summary than necessary and often **replace insight with simple commentary**. Although the **purpose** of the text and the **strategies** are stated, they are **both superficial**, and lack substance. Syntax and mechanics are often correct, with small indelicacies, but the verbs may be weak and the language, artless. Big problem: **lacks insight** and summarizes the text too often.

Example (5/6)

Cesar Chavez, labor union organizer and civil rights leader, advocates the practice of non-violence. Citing figures like Martin Luther King (on his holiday) and Gandhi, he lends credibility to his speech by buffing it up with strong examples of leaders and movements that made non-violence work. He also employs a combination of sympathy and logic, playing the sympathetic card for his poor, oppressed group, and bringing back to mind that most "revolutions" wound up giving nothing to those who sacrificed for them.

Chavez starts out brilliantly by using good timing, speaking on the 10th anniversary of Martin Luther King's assassination. Citing actions and legacies of America's greatest campaigner of equality and his inspiration Gandhi he shows that non-violent resistance has already moved mountains across the world. He then goes on to say, "if, for every violent act committed against us, we responded with non-violence, we attract people's support." Sympathy is arguably the most important factor when campaigning for rights, because once people connect with you they see you at the same level "when victory comes through violence, it is a victory with strings attached." This sympathetic appeal strengthens his argument, and the purpose of the text, to present the value and efficacy of non-violent resistance.

He goes on, making his second valuable point: Non-violence isn't flawed, it is simply better by design. Violence brings pain to both sides and eliminates total victory from the equation. He directly addresses this point because he understands his audience, as most audiences, may assume weakness from passive resistance. But the unwillingness to engage does not imply the inability to do so. Chavez uses the many revolutions in the past as examples of successful non-violent protests, because they were non-violent.

In conclusion Chavez validates his union's plan as one which has worked and as the route which brings the most satisfaction. Violence is a faulty and patchwork solution to a problem which needs to be rebuilt from the ground up.

Grading Practice

This section offers a selection of Rhetorical Analysis essays for your review. These essay address different prompts (which should become clear in their respective theses), and contain moments with writing errors and indelicacies, as well as artful and articulate moments. Take into consideration everything you've learned from this part of the book and score the following essays, as best you can. Remember that these essays were written under "40 minutes" (as would be the case the day of the test), and so should be rewarded for what they do right, not so much penalized for what they do wrong. If an essay doesn't seem to fit one score, give it two; chances are that the essay exceeds the criteria for one score (say 5), but does not quite meet the criteria for a higher score (say 6). This can happen, but try your best to assign each essay a single score. After you score each one, you'll find an answer page after all the essays.

Scoring Guidelines

9 Highly Effective
These essays have everything in the description of an 8, but are deliberately provocative in language, seductively alluring with creativity and just sexy all together with personality. These essays make you go back for seconds.

8 Effective
These essays offer original insight and elaborate extensively, with creative introductions and meaningful conclusions, all the while using sophisticated language. They go beyond general commentary, quoting the text, often blending quotations with their sentences. Most importantly, these essays make compelling connections between the writer's strategies and their effect on the overall purpose of the text.

7 More than Adequate
These essays meet the criteria of a 6, but they offer more insight and better examples. Often times, these essays include elaborate sentence structures which greatly facilitate reading them.

6 Adequate
These essays get the job done: presenting a clear thesis, though not particularly sophisticated, and organizing focused ideas in developed paragraphs. However, they may offer sufficiently developed textual examples, with less detailed and/or less convincing superficial explanations. These essays provide more summary than necessary and often replaces insight with simple commentary. Syntax and mechanics are often correct, with small indelicacies, but the verbs may be weak and the language, artless. Big problem: lacks insight.

5 Almost Adequate
These essays are more than inadequate but not impressive enough to earn a 6. The thesis contains minimal analysis, with an unspecified claim, the bodies feel like summaries with some commentary and quotations that are not expanded on. These essays are just superficial. There is an attempt at organization, Intro, Body, Conclusion, but there are too many redundancies, vague verbs, and simple vocabulary.

4 Inadequate
These essays are unacceptable. There is no real thesis, just a restatement of the prompt, without valid or with weak evidence; the introductions don't offer any real direction for the rest of the essay. The body paragraphs basically summarize, offer little or no textual evidence, with an immature reading or analysis of the text. Generally, these essays don't advance any ideas or settle any conversations; they're boring, unimaginative, and repetitive.

3-2 Little Success

Rhetorical Analysis Essay #1

It is held by all Americans that all men are created equal and freedom must be fought for and protected. Alfred Green's speech in 1861 advocates these principles by urging his African American audience to campaign for the right to participate in the Civil War. Green constantly refines his argument and confronts the counter arguments, in order to ignite a determination in his audience to earn the ability to fight for the equality granted to all men and to abolish the "tyrant system of slavery."

Green prompts his fellow African Americans to transcend from their indignation in an endeavor to cease their focus on the past and transition them to a state of hope for the future. He acknowledges that "the brave deeds of our [founding] fathers...have failed to bring us into recognition as citizens..." to anticipate the objections of his audience, and thus strengthen his position and earn credibility. Furthermore, by conceding the grievances faced by African Americans in the past, he can then arrive at his claim that only by moving forward and assisting in the war efforts can they earn their freedom and change the future of all blacks.

Throughout the entirety of his speech, Green redefines his rationale for African American contribution in the war to better suit his audience. He voices that African Americans should want to participate to "give evidence... of the bravery and patriotism of a race in whose hearts burns the love of [this] country..." to establish patriotism as a basis for his claim. He continues by stating "[it is] our duty, brethren..." to augment his argument by including responsibility as a reason for fighting in the war. He then makes one final revision by incorporating the prospect of abolishing slavery to entice his audience into embracing the idea of petitioning for the ability to join the Union forces.

Alfred Green's speech effectively persuades his reluctant audience to take action and defend their innate rights as human beings. Freedom must be fought for and protected, for once it is lost it can never be recovered.

What score would you give it? _____

Rhetorical Analysis Essay # 2

A mother's instinct is to help her child achieve their full potential, no matter the cost. This quintessential ideal is evident in Samuel Johnson's response to a mother who had previously implored him to ask the prestigious Archbishop of Canterbury for his patronage of her son's university tuition. Johnson rejects the woman, and pens this missive to offer her his reasoning, advice, condolences due to the emotionally-fraught situation. The author lets her down easy and rationally through making it known that she overstepped her boundaries through her failed appeal to authority, and by employing a stern, yet sensitive tone and diction to ease her heightened emotional state.

In paragraph 2, Samuel Johnson addresses the woman's prior appeal to him, and refutes her logic, plainly explaining to her that she overstepped her boundary in addressing him. Johnson states "You ask me to solicit a great man, to whom I never spoke, for a young person whom I had never seen, upon a supposition which I had no means of knowing to be true" (Line 17). The author makes it evident to the woman that she has asked too much of him; she personally asks Johnson, an esteemed English orator and philosopher, to speak to the leader of the Canterbury sect of the Catholic Church, an extremely prestigious position in the 18th century when the church held a very important place in everyday life, to speak on behalf of a student of whom he has no knowledge of. She is asking him to risk his reputation, in the case that Canterbury refuses him, in order to provide for a child, he has no connection with. He addresses the previous statement in Line 30, "there is no reason why that should be done by me, without some particular relation to both the

Archbishop and you." This awkward situation is what Johnson employs to reason his dismissal of the woman's son; he cannot accurate provide a report of her and neither can the bishop, despite their high positions. And their lofty positions is what she aspires will help her son; she assumes that with both Johnson and the Archbishop on her son's side, he will make it into the university. Johnson rebuffs the woman's irrational faith in both himself and the Archbishop with his own rationality.

Samuel Johnson conducts the letter with sever yet understanding tone, in order to assuage the woman of his understanding, coupled with a sentence structure that progressively gets to the point, as to not overwhelm her with his startling rejection. He begins the letter by out rightly stating his reluctance to pen the letter, to avoid "destroying any hope" the woman holds, appearing terse (4). He then pontificates on the woman's hope, explaining the flightiness and "pain" that hope and love can cause, thus addressing the false sense of hope instilled in her, in regards to Johnson himself, and easing her into the nail in the coffin; rejection (7). By beating around the bush, Johnson addresses her concern and validates her experience while simultaneously dismantling her ideals. Samuel Johnson ends the letter by warmly addressing the woman's pure intention of helping her son and develops an apologetic tone; "If I could help you by any proper means it would give me pleasure (30-32). Johnson says this to the woman to give an alternative to the present situation; he would have helped her son, if she would have approached him in an appropriate and timely manner, and would have been happy to help, thus appealing to her emotionally. Furthermore, he compliments her son, remarking that he is a "pretty youth" and wishes that "he may still be wise, youthful and happy, thus validating her reason for writing the letter in the first place: her son's merit (36-39). The author maintains a considerate yet admonishing tone in order to correct the woman's behavior and appear benevolent and understanding.

English orator Samuel Johnson's address of maternal concern is a timeless evocation of a parent's love for their child. This promotion of a step away from children's affair proves true today, as many parents live vicariously through their children's lives, and are extremely hesitant about allowing children to go to college without them, fretting about if they've done enough to prepare their progeny for the future.

What score would you give it? _____

Rhetorical Analysis Essay #3

For most countries, the advent of the Internet and the technological revolution of the 20th century brought intellectual pursuit to the forefront of innovation and led to increasing respect for the intelligentsia. However, American persecution of intellectuals has been perpetuated, despite these advancements. In his article "America Needs its Nerds" author Leonid Fridman questions these antiquated views still held by many Americans. Fridman criticizes American values of anti-intellectualism by making cross-cultural comparisons to illustrate the absurdity of American ideals and using figurative language to emphasize the consequences of such ideals.

Fridman juxtaposes American views on intelligence with those of other nations to show the absurdity of the American perspective, claiming that "anti-intellectualism runs higher in American popular culture then it does anywhere else in the world" (line 36-37). He supports this claim by referencing the East Asian emphasis on academics and education, saying that a studious and intelligent child is "lauded," while that same child in America would be ridiculed, labeled a geek or nerd (line 1-4, 37-40). He further bolsters his argument by noting that in the U.S., faculty of the most Prestigious universities are respected and paid less than a mediocre athlete, an phenomenon unheard of in foreign countries (lines 41-46). Through these comparisons, Friedman illustrates the backwardness of American values and taps into a word version of American exceptionalism, emphasizing the antiquity and inferiority of America societal views in relation to the countless countries that prize intelligence.

Employing a variety of figurative language, Fridman emphasizes the detriment of these ideals. He introduces the ironic example of Harvard University in line 11, saying that despite its status as a vanguard of an intellectual advancement, Harvard nevertheless holds deep-seeded into intellectual values with students who emphasize academics being intimidated in overshadowed by star athlete (line 11-18). This demonstrates the pervasiveness of fallacious American values and serves as an analogy for Fridman's arguments that compares Harvard to the U.S., both holding views that run counter to their prestige and status. In the last paragraph, Fridman asks two rhetorical questions. Both concern American views and their impact on the world, saying that a country that ridicules the intellectually motivated can't possibly maintain its Socio-political influence or its standing as a global power (lines 47-56).

By incorporating these rhetorical questions, Fridman forces readers to reevaluate their opinions on intellectualism and appeals to the American competitive spirit, demonstrating that these prejudices erode the countries impact on a global scale. By questioning American antagonism of intellectuals, Friedman seeks to change these long-standing views and implement superior ones in their place arguing that by ostracizing the intellectually inclined and academically motivated, Americas is only ostracizing itself from a more tolerant and accepting world.

What score would you give it? _____

Scores

Rhetorical Analysis Essay #1 - score 6, 7

Rhetorical Analysis Essay #2 - score 7

Rhetorical Analysis Essay #3 - score 8

A WORD ON SYNTHESIS

An AP English Language and Composition Synthesis essay is essentially a **short research paper**, in which you make an argument that takes a specific **stance** on a topic, using your **research** as support for your claims. Unlike Rhetorical Analysis, which demands a "breaking down" in order to achieve meaning, Synthesis demands that you "bring the parts together" in order to make meaning. The parts, of course, constitute your research, which added to the claim(s) your research supports, would make it the whole.

The Synthesis essay is demanding in the way it calls for a well-researched argument that considers a multiplicity of views. So here are some,

Key distinctions of the Synthesis Essay

1. You are making an argument, but it's not a fight. The synthesis essay should be less claim-based and more claim-driven.

2. Claim-driven essays have a clear idea they favor and endeavor to show just that by incorporating research, while **claim-based** essays function as series of claims, all sub-related to the main claim, that rely on examples and explanations to prove their merit. The latter usually becomes the basis for argumentative writing.

3. You're not "arguing," but **you are making an argument**. Don't approach the prompt (or issue) with a lazy "he's right and she's right and there is not truth in the universe" attitude. Your essay must take a specific stance.

4. Your stance should be an 80/20 percent, where your points has merit or value 80% of the time or your point is the best solution to the problem 80% of the time, while the other point(s) have merit or value sometimes (that constitutes 20% of the time), but definitely not enough to make it the better solution.

5. There aren't two sides to an argument; whoever taught you that, lied to you. There are many (numerous [too many to count]) sides to an argument. Your argument is stronger when you consider as many of them as you can.

6. Your relationship with your sources should be 50/50 percent. You speak 50% of the time and they speak the other 50%. However, limit their involvement in your essay to only the body paragraphs. Quotations in the intro make it seem like you're handing the baton too soon, and quotations at the end give the impression that they get the last word. Always speak first and last.

7. Don't crowd out the sources with too many of your claims, **but don't let them run the show either.** If you only bring in the sources for yes sir," or "yes ma'am," it will imply minimal engagement with the sources and engagement with the sources is the whole point of Synthesis writing.

Synthesis, Not Rhetorical

The **Rhetorical Analysis** essay has a much more organized, and sometimes "prescribed" format of composition than the **Synthesis** essay. And while general practices of good writing transfer from one essay to another, the following differences should be observed:

- Insightful writing is usually the byproduct of "good reading" in Rhetorical Analysis. **Synthesis**, on the other hand, provides six sources and 15 minutes to read them. You simply **don't have the time** to engage with each of the Synthesis sources the way you engage with the Rhetorical text.

- Rhetorical Analysis asks you to evaluate how successful a text is at making its point. **Synthesis doesn't do that.** Whatever points are made in those sources, are **points you can appropriate for your own essay**, for your own purpose.

- One implied assumption of the Rhetorical Analysis text is that the text the college board provides for you is good, rich with rhetorical strategies and devices for you to analyze. **Don't make that assumption** with the Synthesis sources. The sources assigned in Synthesis **can be flawed**, have logical fallacies or weak evidence. So be selective.

Synthesis, Not Argumentative

These distinctions point out just how different Synthesis and Argumentative are, and yet how often they cross paths. However, the aforementioned distinctions refer to **approach**, while the ones that follow concern differences in complexity:

- Argumentative essays (especially true of AP Language and Composition) usually demand a more philosophical engagement, either with meaningful quotations or theories, **while Synthesis essays usually deal with a particular issue, or problem that concerns everyday living** (examples to follow).

- Argumentative essays welcome most evidence outside of the given text, such as historical examples or anecdotes, while **Synthesis essays insist on relying on the sources provided**, as evidence to the argument.

- Argumentative essays use evidence to strengthen their claims (after all, they are claim-driven), but **Synthesis essays build claims off of evidence**. Meaning, Synthesis essays have a habit of arriving at claims or building extended claims after a careful consideration of the evidence.

A Conversation with the Text

AP English Language and Composition teachers like to describe the Synthesis essay as having a conversation with the text. The implication does not refer to the reading of the sources; instead, the idea is that the writing (your essay) should feel like a conversation with the text.

...feel like a conversation with the text

> **Try not to be stiff.** It's easy to make a point, use a quotation, and move on. It's harder and better to weave that point through the tapestry of evidence.
> <u>Example</u> "Source C says..." "While Source B confirms..."
>
> **Be relaxed** instead. There should be a fluidity from one quotation to another.
> <u>Example</u> "Erick Hoffman's metaphoric phrasing of global affairs as "currency illiteracy" (C) is certainly echoed by Bateman's New York Times column, "The Language of Money," (B) where he considers, like Hoffman, that "an understanding of language and the culture that comes with it" (C) is an indicator of success in a "business world where an exchange of words precedes an exchange of money" (B).

A conversation with the text demonstrates you understand the sources so well – their purpose, their biases and implications so well – that you are able to moderate and participate in a conversation between them, as you would between friends. But in order to do that well, you should...

keep the following things in mind:

Accuracy

- Report information from different sources, demonstrating an **adequate understanding of the purpose** of each source.

- Quote or paraphrase information from the sources, in a way that **does not misconstrue the meaning** of the material referenced.

- Use information from the sources, **without fabricating information** not found in the source indicated.

Organization

- Structure quotations and paraphrases in a way that **each source receives attribution** for the information they contribute.

- Arrange the material referenced in a way that readers can instantly **see how the sources work together** to make complete meaning.

Explanation

- Your essay should **explain and expand on the ramifications** of the sources in such a way that the readers understand their complexities.

- You must **make the sources make sense** by pretending that the reader hasn't read the sources and therefore needs background information to understand them better. However, be careful not to trade insightful explanation for mere summarization.

READING THE PROMPT

<u>The recommendations are:</u>

- to **read the prompt** once BEFORE reading the sources and once more AFTER reading the sources. If you don't read it before, you'll have difficulty focusing the sources' scattered conversations on one specific issue, and if you don't read it after, you may mistake the sources' conversation with the task you were given. Remember, **the sources NEVER answer the prompt**; that's your job.

- to **identify the type of claim** the prompt is asking for, usually: either a **Claim of Policy** (offer a solution/recommendation, considering whether this should be established, or if that should be changed) or a **Claim of Value** (sometimes as simple as good/bad, but more often, developing a stance this issue, whether for/against something). Remember that Policy and Value often go hand in hand.

The task assigned in a Synthesis essay is often relatively simple, and mistaken as simple, so reduced to simple arguments. However, students must **recognize the complexity of the issue** before they begin composing their responses; the task may be "easy," but your task isn't. Writers are rewarded when they recognize this complexity and write accordingly.

A Look at the Synthesis Question

AP ENGLISH LANGUAGE AND COMPOSITION SAMPLE
RESPONSE
Question 1
(Suggested time—40 minutes)

This paragraph offers <u>context and background</u> for the task the next paragraph will ask. Pay close attention to the things this paragraph chooses to include and exclude because it <u>delineates the parameters of the conversation</u>. Whatever is in this paragraph relates to the sources, sometimes only minimally because the sources have their own purposes and they don't usually answer the prompt completely.

This paragraph will tell you to read and choose at least three sources (I recommend four) as evidence to your well-developed argument that evaluates _____. This verb can sometimes be "evaluates," or "considers," "examines," "take a position on," and more recently (2016 prompt) "argues." Nonetheless, the language of <u>the prompt always invites conversation</u>.

This paragraph will tell you to remain focused, to be clear and to <u>use the sources</u> to "develop your argument and [its] reasoning." It will also tell you how to cite (using Source A, etc.), and imply that you quote from the sources in a variety of way: direct quotation, paraphrase or summary (short summary).

This section details the sources you are to read:
A, B, C, D, E, F and sometimes G.

Prompt Example

Imagine that a **Synthesis essay prompt** asked whether people who know one language are at a disadvantage over those who are bilingual.

The reasons and evidence come from the sources, so these will become clearer as you read them. Instead, the first concern when reading the prompt is to determine a **claim** – a definitive stance on the prompt. This stance cannot be something simple.

Simple

Question? Are speakers of one language at a disadvantage? Answer? Yes, they are, because ____, or no they are not, because [insert source quotation here].

A simple response to the prompt may turn the essay into an argumentative essay, as opposed to a synthesis essay, and perhaps not even a good one. Instead, Synthesis essay writing calls for something more polished, more complex.

Complex

<u>Are people who only know one language at a disadvantage?</u>
First, I'd have to read the sources before committing to any assertion, but at a glance, they do seem to be. The world is so interconnected, that now more than ever, we must know other languages in order to succeed in the business world.

<u>But are they at a disadvantage or is it just that they don't have an advantage?</u>
Well, not a disadvantage, per say, because if the person knows English, which (the sources will say) is a dominant language in the world's financial and political spheres, then that person may not be at a disadvantage.

<u>So, are they at an advantage?</u>
No, because other countries are improving, and their people are learning other languages (which would facilitate commerce, etc.) so if they are improving, so should the people who only know one language. Perhaps they are not at a disadvantage in their own country, but they are at a disadvantage internationally.

So, the final product should be a **sophisticated claim** that answers the prompt and still takes an **original and definitive** stance.

Sophisticated

People who understand and speak different languages are more likely to be successful in fields like business, commerce and hospitality because...

<u>Now it's time to read the sources.</u>

READING THE TEXT

Tips for Dealing with the Sources

- **The sources will be brief** and will vary: opinion piece, newspaper article, research excerpt, some graphic (picture, political cartoon, etc.), a table or graph on pertinent information. Don't just use all the newspaper articles; show diversity.

- **Must you read them ALL?** No. Should you? Yes. All in detail? No. Scan the source subheading and the first paragraph to determine if the source will be useful in your essay. You only have 15 minutes, so use your time wisely.

- **Not all sources have the same merit.** Some will be opinion-based, like "why the Honor Code works in my school," and these sources will only be useful with that specificity ("in my school") in mind. Certainly, an article from an online education journal will carry more weight in your essay about honor codes.

- It is crucial that you **understand the source you decide to use.** If you misinterpret the source's argument, your quotations may be out of context. This is especially true when analyzing visuals, like political cartoons; the conclusions you draw from the image must be in line with their intended purpose.

- **Annotate as you read**; some do so in the margins (can be messy), while others write in a separate sheet (easier to record what you mean). Identify if source is pro or con for quick reference later. Underline interesting language in the source you'd like to use in your essay. Note sentences you'd like to quote in your essay.

- **Note source heading**: Commentary column vs. newspaper article? To strengthen your argument, maybe use the language from the first (when explaining) and quote the second (for legitimate evidence). Does the title suggest anything about its purpose/agenda?

- **The sources and the prompt have different purposes.** The key is to differentiate their purpose from your own (which is in response to the prompt) in order to write clearly. In most cases, be careful when appropriating their claims as your own.

WRITING THE ESSAY

There are different modes of composition, especially for a Synthesis essay, but here are some things to consider:

Before Writing the Synthesis Essay

1. Narrow your Focus

Pay attention to the key words in the prompt. It usually instructs to develop a position on something. This position should be sophisticated. Not, "this is right because..." or "this is wrong because..." but rather, a specific stance that moves beyond a simple pro or con response.

2. Choose Sources

Quickly select two or three sources that can really contribute claims and discussion to your essay. If possible, also select the ones that will contribute a quote or a passing reference. Remember these are preliminary choices only; you can always change your mind when it's time to write.

3. Tentative Thesis Statement

An introduction often flows out of the writer's attempt to compose a thesis statement. Use the (first) rough draft as elements of your intro once you begin writing, and when you do, a better thesis will emerge.

4. Simple Outline

Decide what you will talk about first, second and third. That's it.

When Writing the Essay

The most important part of composing a Synthesis essay is to structure it in such a way that others can evaluate the sources, as you present them, and **conclude that your conclusion is sound.**

Quick Tips:

- **Elements from the prompt** can help your write the introduction.

- Make sure your **thesis takes a stance** (not too argumentative and not neutral).

- Reference **no more than two or three sources per body** and no more than four sources as a whole (which is not to say you can't quote more than 4 times).

- Vary your references to the source. Body paragraphs should: use a **summary** to condense a source to no more than a sentence, a **paraphrase** to transpose a paragraph from the source into your own, original words, and use **quotations** (no more than two per body), of source sections no longer than a line and a half.

- **Truly engage with the sources**, by making inferences from their claims and examples, while connecting them (if possible) to points made in other sources.

INTRODUCTION

1ˢᵗ Establish **the topic of the essay** (see 1ˢᵗ paragraph of prompt)

Throughout the last decade, lawmakers and individuals around the country, have proposed **eliminating** a piece of the nation's history: the **penny**.

2ⁿᵈ Contextualize the conversation and establish **stance** (use 1ˢᵗ paragraph of prompt)

Proponents for the discontinuing of the penny, argue that this coin costs the economy more than what it contributes to it, whereas those who advocate for keeping the penny, contend that it is an **integral part of U.S. history**.

3ʳᵈ Present your **thesis** (refer to the task in the 2ⁿᵈ paragraph of prompt)

Yet, the **penny** does contribute to the U.S. economy in various **beneficial** ways, such as job creation and solvency, and it is a relic of our nation's past, therefore it **should be maintained** as the lowest value coin in our economy.

Complete Introduction Example

Throughout the last decade, lawmakers and individuals around the country, have proposed eliminating a piece of the nation's history: the penny. Proponents for the elimination of the penny, argue that this coin costs the economy more than what it contributes to it. Whereas those who advocate for keeping the penny, contend that it is an integral part of U.S. history. Yet, the penny does contribute to the U.S. economy in various beneficial ways , such as job creation and solvency, and is a relic of our nation's past, therefore it should be maintained as the lowest value coin in our economy.

BODY

Body paragraphs **GENERALLY** do the following:

A. Begin with a **claim** that stems from the thesis. This claim becomes the main focus of this body paragraph and should be broad enough to encourage discussion, yet narrow enough to close in conversation by the end of the paragraph.

B. Dedicate the middle portion of the paragraph to the source material, in order to **support** that claim,
- by **quoting**, while offering analysis of the quotation, paraphrasing,
- and briefly **summarizing**,
- all the while, presenting parenthetical **citations** (Source A, B, etc.)

C. End with an **insightful** sentence: that connects to the opening claim and further validates the thesis.

The following section will cover, **SPECIFICALLY** how to execute these steps and compose a strong (not flawless) body paragraph. The steps outlined need not be followed in the order they are presented; the key is for most of those steps to be present in a Synthesis body paragraph for the composition of a thorough and complex paragraph.

1st The topical sentence of the body concerns **one reason in defense of your thesis**

Pennies are **relics of American history** that embody the progression and development of American **nationalism** and ideology.

2nd Present evidence from source

Prior to 1909, coins simply depicted a random head with the word liberty inscribed on top **(Source G)**.

3rd Explain evidence

After 1909, however, the penny revolutionized the face of American currency, when it featured an actual historical figure who **transformed American thought**: Abraham Lincoln. Lincoln, who was essential in maintaining the unity of the nation throughout a Civil War that threatened to split our great country in 2, **embodies the American spirit** of perseverance.

4th Present evidence from another source

In fact, this shift in image symbolized the "preservation of the U.S. as a single and united country" **(Source F)**.

5th Relate evidence to previous explanation

Thus, **it exemplifies the constancy of America** as a country of freedom and opportunity...

6th Connect the evidences provided, and relate them to the topical claim presented in the first sentence

...and contributes to American nationalistic ideals of pride in our ability to **value collective freedom over discrepancies** in individual ideals.

7th Offer insight, by considering the significance or by explaining the relevance of the conversation thus far, to the thesis presented in the introduction

In short, the **penny revolutionized American currency**, by honoring historical figures unique to America's past, who have helped define it and remind us of what it stands for.

Complete Body Example

Pennies are relics of American history that embody the progression and development of American nationalism and ideology. Prior to 1909, coins simply depicted a random head with the word liberty inscribed on top (Source G). After 1909, however, the penny revolutionized the face of American currency, when it featured an actual historical figure who transformed American thought: Abraham Lincoln. Lincoln, who was essential in maintaining the unity of the nation throughout a Civil War that threatened to split our great country in 2, embodies the American spirit of perseverance. In fact, this shift in image symbolized the "preservation of the U.S. as a single and united country" (Source F). Thus, it exemplifies the maintenance of America as a country of freedom and opportunity and contributes to American nationalistic ideals of pride in our ability to value collective freedom over discrepancies in individual ideals. In short, the penny revolutionized American currency, by honoring historical figures unique to America's past, who have helped define it and remind us of what it stands for.

CONCLUSION

1ˢᵗ Final thoughts on how the evidence presented in your bodies supports your thesis.

Beyond its economic benefits and respected history, the **penny has a place in American currency** because it stands as a symbol of liberty through adversity.

2ⁿᵈ Slow down your essay. **Begin the end.**

Such a small coin, and yet it carries the imprint of American values, an emblem of tradition...

3ʳᵈ Draw **final insight** from the information presented.

...to remind us of our past and **help us preserve our future**.

Complete Conclusion Example

Beyond its economic benefits and respected history, the penny has a place in American currency because it stands as a symbol of liberty through adversity. Such a small coin, and yet it carries the imprint of American values, an emblem of tradition - to remind us of our past and help us preserve our future.

PACING THE ESSAY
(15 mins. Reading + 40 mins. Writing)

What follows is a recommended timetable for the composition of the Synthesis essay, within the allotted time of 40 minutes of writing + 15 minutes of reading. While the timing and process of composition will vary from writer to writer, the breakdown below offers **a realistic and effective approach** to use the day of the test.

15 Minutes

(The Prompt)

1. Read the prompt carefully, in the order of paragraphs: (1) the **context**, so you can frame the discussion, (2) the **task**, so you understand what is being asked and (3) the **writing specifications**, so you are reminded of the expectations your readers will have from your essay.

(The Sources)

1. Take your time reading the sources, but always, **be selective**. Not all the sources will prove useful or crucial to your essay.

2. Take careful notes of the sources or sections of sources you plan to use, but **don't re-read** whole texts after you begin your essay.

3. I recommend you **don't begin writing until you have used the fifteen minutes**, reading the sources. Once you begin the essay, you won't have sufficient time to go back and forth between the passages and the essay without compromising the organization and clarity of your essay.

4. Analyze **the argument and purpose of the source**. Examine the claims and the evidence they use to support them. Identify the biases implied in the texts.

35 Minutes

(The Essay)

1. **Write out your thesis**; chances are that your introduction will flow out of it. The thesis should turn the task of the prompt into a claim and use the sources' own evidence as your support.

2. **Plan your essay.** A well-planned essay is always more organized, focused and easier to compose. Don't over plan either.

3. Synthesis essays have the danger of becoming chatty, so make sure you: (1) **don't deviate** into personal experiences or your own ruminations on the topic, and (2) do **connect your claims** to the evidence you use to support them.

4. To show diversity, offer a variety of **quotations**, **paraphrasing**, and **summarization**. A few of the first, less of the second, and really only one of the third.

5. Explain everything you quote; make meaning of the references for the reader.

5 minutes

(The revision)

1. Proofread your essay, looking for missing citations, correcting quotation marks and to ensure you've quoted at least 3 different sources, at least 4 times. **Worry about the simple things you can fix.**

Complete Synthesis Essay Examples

This section includes a selection of Synthesis essays; each scored, like many of the paragraphs presented beforehand, ranging from mid to high. I decided not to include low-scoring essays because their glaring issues often make them easier to recognize. So I included essays that are neither all good nor all bad, instead, they are - each of them - good and bad; some with laudable moments in the writing, and others with page-tearing-what-were-you-thinking moments. Not only does this varying quality makes them more challenging to score, but realistically, that is how essays are written, with good, bad, and ugly moments.

Disclaimer
Since Synthesis essays depend on textual sources for information to accomplish and succeed in their intended task, the student sample essays that follow will, similarly, quote from different sources, from time to time, which will not be included in this book.

Essay #1

As Americans, we have one shared goal: to keep the United States ahead of competing nations. Unfortunately, this cannot be done with less and less children being educated in a foreign language. This puts us at a disadvantage, a disadvantage that can be addressed by teaching future and current generations new languages to keep the U.S. competitive in the global market and international affairs, and to better stimulate our children's minds to create a mentally active population.

According to the United States Census Bureau, around only 20% of the U.S. population aged 5 years or older speaks a language other than English at home. This is an alarmingly low percentage that has raised the attention of many people, including author Richard Haass. Haass claims that by not teaching students useful languages like Arabic, the United States is less prepared to handle national security affairs. This statement highlights the idea that monolingualism not only puts someone at a disadvantage, but it also casts them as ill-prepared for any adversity that may come from abroad. Furthermore, a lack of multilingualism is hurting our position in an increasingly voracious global market. David Thomas of the Associated Newspapers points out that, "fewer and fewer of [Americans] are learning a foreign language, while more and more foreigners become multi-lingual." This gives monolinguals one clear choice: to become educated in a new, useful language. Learning a new language will allow Americans to be better equipped in confronting economic rivals and give the U.S. a better view of "global perspectives," as Catherine Porter of the Modern Language Association describes it.

Besides being helpful to the country, multi-lingualism also allows one's brain to be constantly at work. Ursula Oaks, author of "Foreign-Language Learning: What the United States is Missing Out On," describes using multiple languages as a "mental jog on the treadmill: strangely energized, brainstretched, more ready for any challenge." This implies reaching the state of an active mind, which allows for more productive problem solving and innovative thinking. In fact, Russell Berman ("Foreign Language for Foreign Policy?") states that learning a second language can also increase one's understanding of their first language, dispelling the notion that monolinguals have better control of their first language due to a singular focus. Berman furthers this idea by adding that, "With the core language skills...come higher-order capacities." This signals that by exposing one's self to new languages, one can unlock a higher understanding that will ultimately help in everyday endeavors.

Overall, in this day and age, a monolingual English speaker holds only disadvantages when compared to their more cultured counterparts. With more to access to global affairs, and a better understanding of fundamental language, multi-linguals have become the new standard of a world class citizen.

(Score 8, 9)

Essay #2

Throughout history, innovation and progress has arisen from the human being's instinctive desire to explore the unknown. After discovering nearly all of the Earth's surface, humanity's unquenchable hunger for exploration has propelled them towards space in attempts to establish extraterrestrial colonies. Some critics contend that such explorations have ethical and financial consequences that should be considered before additional funding is attributed to space exploration. What the opposition fails to consider however, is the vast impact of space exploration on advancing technological research, unifying countries and the world alike, and creating jobs for Americas. Therefore, when discussing funding for space exploration, these economic and social benefits should be considered.

Space exploration's ability to advance technological research, and unify countries and the world alike is a decisive factor when making decisions about space exploration. In order to launch humans and space probes into space, adequate technology is necessary. The technology necessary for space exploration was not around when the program first started, so innovation and intuition were necessary to build adequate machinery. As a result, the fields of astronomy, physics, and mathematics expanded as rockets, satellites, telescopes, and countless other technologies were developed. This is demonstrated in Source B where a rocket is depicted: without the competition and promise generated by space exploration, such revolutionary technology would not exist. Therefore, individuals who are determining how much resources should be invested in space programs, should consider the fact that they have largely contributed to the development of science and technology and possess the ability to further revolutionize these fields. Space exploration has also been accompanied by global collaboration, as it requires "getting people together to work out joint solutions" (Source G). In order to maximize space technology, various countries have to work together to conduct the elaborate experiments that test out astronomical concepts. The technology, innovation, and experimentation that space exploration requires, demands global collaboration, and possesses the ability to incite competitive improvement and unity amongst all nations.

When making decisions about space exploration, its ability to yield a vast array of occupations and wealth for a nation, should be considered. In order to create the satellites, rockets, and other equipment used in intergalactic journeys, mathematicians and scientists are needed. In fact, the money that is spent on space programs goes towards "manufacturing, research and development, salaries, doctors, scientists, teachers, and corporations" (Source A). By providing an array of occupations for individuals, astronomical research greatly contributes to the economy: the more people working these well-paying jobs, the more affluence generated by these individuals and consequently the government who benefits when individuals have the means to sustain themselves and contribute to the economy. Space exploration also boosts academic pursuit, as it provides "hope and inspiration for youngsters who are growing up doing schoolwork" (Source A). Space has an alluring intrigue that promotes youth's pursuit of careers in this field. With increasingly more individuals involving themselves in interstellar exploration, this field is rapidly becoming a force for employment, so when determining how many resources should be invested in space programs, the fact that it is rapidly expanding and becoming a powerhouse for employment should be considered. As mentioned previously, with more available jobs comes more economic development, so naturally the expansion of space exploration has the potential to yield huge economic benefits. One may argue that the funding spent on space exploration is exorbitant and best spent on medical research and domestic programs. However, less than six cents of American taxes are currently spent on space and technology when compared to the ten cents invested in health (Source C). In reality, space research does not have an enormous economic toll on the economy and given all the success it has already generated in sending men to the moon and its beneficial input into the economy, it is a field that possesses the ability to revolutionize science and society.

Space exploration is the means through which technological advancements, economic development, and unification can be achieved: inevitably it is the technology of the present and the future, so when considering how much funding it should receive, these factors should be considered. Space exploration has become the catalyst that promotes innovative competition and development; it is only a matter of time before all nations realize that for societies to progress, resources must be contributed to this program.

(Score 8, 9)

Essay #3

College is an experience that some say everyone should enroll in, boasting the positive impacts of advancement of knowledge as well as the amount of social growth and development one receives. There are, however, several negatives associated with college, with its sheer cost at the top of the list. The cost of college has proved to not always outweigh its benefits, and some would argue that the experience doesn't teach life skills required to survive in the real world.

While college itself offers an education that is unmatched by any other institution, the cost of such education is not worth it for many students. Source E retains that "students today are taking on more debt...and those factors make higher education a risky investment," and some cannot afford said investment; many say that the education system falls short at providing realistic value for the money that they spend and that college is just too expensive for them to afford (Source F). Monetary costs hold people back from their true potential and are just not realistic in modern times.

The cost of college is not just monetary. Skills like innovation and judgement cannot be taught. Source B says, "it no longer makes sense to devote four years of higher education entirely to specific skills," implying that self-application will always be the best education and it starts with the person. An economist in Source A argues that the distinction within the labor market is not between the more or less educated, but of the concrete services that one supplies. In both resources, it can be emphasized that people contain the skills needed to succeed, and these skills have no price. Success has nothing to do with education, but it has everything to do with the person.

College is altogether an expensive affair that not everyone can enjoy or afford. It can prove to be a waste of energy and resources if you find out that all you need are things that you already had – passion, drive, and a small loan of $1million from your daddy.

(Score 5, 6)

The Almost Adequate Essay

One of the most difficult essays, and one of my most commonly scored essays, is the **5/6 essay**. This is the essay that stands in the threshold of inadequate (4) and could've entered into adequate (6), but it isn't bad enough to be the former nor good enough to be the latter. These can be a challenge. The key is to remember what adequate essays read like:

6 Adequate
These essays **get the job done**: presenting a **clear thesis**, though **not** particularly **sophisticated**, and organizing **focused ideas** in developed paragraphs. However, they may offer **sufficiently** developed **textual examples**, with less detailed and/or less convincing **superficial explanations**. These essays provide more summary than necessary and often **replace insight with simple commentary**. They may also reference the texts, directly or indirectly, but not in any significant or meaningful way, and **only once or twice a paragraph**, offering **some analysis** of the quotations. Syntax and mechanics are often correct, with small indelicacies, but the verbs may be weak and the language, artless. Big problem: lacks insight.

Example (5/6)

The English language, although it is spoken by the majority of the world's population can be found to be a hindrance for those who only choose to abide by it. While the rest of the world already has at least their native tongue and English under their belt, English monolinguals will find themselves at a disadvantage to only speak one language. Learning other languages will be more beneficial economically and connect the country to others as well as for the nation benefiting people personally.

Understanding and speaking another country's language can help the U.S. gain more financially. "Language [is] a gateway to Global communities states Haass (source A). Through language, the nation can have a better national security, economy and foreign policy. Other nations are learning the language of the countries they're trading with so they can better communicate with them not only physically, but culturally as well leaders in government and policy continue to live in a bubble of their own making imagining that we can be global while refusing to learn the languages or learn about the culture of the rest of the world," (source A). For the United States to choose to be ignorant and pretend like English is the most well-known language around will only harm the country as a whole while other competitors sever the ties the U.S. holds on other countries and take it for themselves one sentence at a time. Little Englanders, to a life of dismal isolation while an educated, sophisticated Euro-competitor is chat away to foreign customers and steal all our business as a result," (source B). Although English is the most predominant language, nothing ever stays on top and when the language does get dethroned, multilingual speakers and countries will find themselves with an upper hand while the U.S. falls rock bottom.

Language is not just a way of speaking, it is all that and more. Through language, people can understand other people's cultures and their way of living. Sometimes phrases can't be translated but only understood in the context of that certain language. In a country made entirely of immigrants as well, the Us would find it in their best interest to be multilingual in order to communicate with their neighbors. The absence of knowing another language is "a devastating waste of potential. students who learn languages at an early age display enhanced cognitive abilities relative to their monolingual peers," (source D). Not only does language connect others socially and culturally, but it benefits people personally as well. Being multilingual, Porter says, makes "the brain more flexible and [incites] it to discover new patterns and thus to create and maintain more circuits" (source D). Multilingualism can only be beneficial for oneself and being a monolingual, only a hindrance not just physically, socially and culturally, but also mentally. The same way monolinguals are more open minded when it comes to learning more than one language, the easier they will be able to adapt to changes while English monolingual continue to neglect other languages and limit only themselves and overall their nation.

Understanding and learning a different language other than English can only be beneficial towards the individual and as a whole, nation. Multi-linguals are more well-rounded. They understand and can better interact with not only foreign countries, but the people living right next door to them. Beneath the surface of language, lies a whole new world, a whole new culture and a whole new way of living that is only understood and perceived by those willing to step out of their comfort zone, and learn.

Grading Practice

This section offers a selection of Synthesis essays for your review. These essay address different prompts (which should become clear in their respective theses), and contain moments with writing errors and indelicacies, as well as artful and articulate moments. Take into consideration everything you've learned from this part of the book and score the following essays, as best you can. Remember that these essays were written under "40 minutes" (as would be the case the day of the test), and so should be rewarded for what they do right, not so much penalized for what they do wrong. If an essay doesn't seem to fit one score, give it two; chances are that the essay exceeds the criteria for one score (say 5), but does not quite meet the criteria for a higher score (say 6). This can happen, but try your best to assign each essay a single score. After you score each one, you'll find an answer page after all the essays.

Scoring Guidelines

9 Highly Effective
These essays have everything in the description of an 8, but show a profound understanding of a nuanced issue, demonstrate a skilled facility in conducting and presenting research and read as if the student-writer was having a conversation with the sources.

8 Effective
These essays offer original insight and elaborate extensively, with creative introductions and meaningful conclusions, all the while using sophisticated language. They go beyond general commentary, quoting the text, often blending quotations with their sentences. Most importantly, these essays make compelling connections between the task in the prompt and the information gathered in the sources, to complete a well-balanced argument.

7 More than Adequate
These essays meet the criteria of a 6, but they offer more insight and better examples. Integration of the sources into the writing is done deliberately and with a notable amount of grace and refinement.

6 Adequate
These essays get the job done: presenting a clear thesis, and organizing focused ideas in developed paragraphs. However, they may offer sufficiently developed textual examples, with less detailed and/or less convincing superficial explanations. These essays provide more summary than necessary and often replaces insight with simple commentary. They may also reference the texts, directly or indirectly, but not in any significant or meaningful way, and only once or twice a paragraph, offering some analysis of the quotations. Syntax and mechanics are often correct, with small indelicacies, but the verbs may be weak and the language, artless. Big problem: lacks insight.

5 Almost Adequate
These essays are more than inadequate (4) but not impressive enough to earn a 6. The thesis contains minimal analysis, with an unspecified claim, the bodies feel like summaries with some commentary and quotations that are not expanded on. These essays are just superficial. There is an attempt at organization, Intro, Body, Conclusion, but there are too many redundancies, vague verbs, and simple vocabulary.

4 Inadequate
These essays are unacceptable. There is no real thesis, just a restatement of the prompt, without valid or with weak evidence; the introductions don't offer any real direction for the rest of the essay. The body paragraphs basically summarize, offer little or no textual evidence, with an immature reading or analysis of the text. Generally, these

essays don't advance any ideas or settle any conversations; they're boring, unimaginative, and repetitive.

3-2 Little Success

Synthesis Essay #1

When thinking of the American dream, college has long been a focal point. And for good reason, college is an investment for the future, that one virtually cannot succeed without. Despite rising costs, attending college remains more advantageous than not attending, and as such, becomes worth its price.

College remains a tenet of the American dream, an expectation for all. In fact, 94% of parents expect their child to attend college (source F). The common adage being that, a college education prepares you for, and presents you with opportunity for, a better future. Most will agree with the need for a college education, and the most common citation for not getting one, is price. While 75% of Americans say they cannot afford college (source F), most colleges are not, in fact, very expensive, despite rising costs. The average yearly cost after financial aid is taken into account is about $2000 (source D), not a bad price for something that, on average, earns its recipients a $20,000 salary increase to those without a degree (source F). That is a value over 10x the initial outlay.

The worth of college is found not just in the degree, but in the experience itself. A "successful liberal arts education develops the capacity for innovation and for judgement" (source B). Rather than training for a specific skill, and be settled to it for life, students become well rounded, productive members of society, so they can "become agents of change...not victims of it" (source B). Even for vocations where a degree is not strictly necessary, those with a college degree have an enormous advantage. Only 33% of young adults get a 4-year degree (source D), and by laws of supply and demand (a need for an educated workforce vs. a limited supply), those with a degree have better chances of employment, which is increasingly necessary, as the unemployment rate rises to 8% and above (source C).

The question asked is "Is college worth its cost?" Often, the case made against a college education is its price and debt it can incur. However, college tuition is shown to have an annual return over 15%, which us more than the historical return for stocks and property combined (source A), making a college education the greatest, and safest, form of investment and speculation you can gamble on in the 21st century. The wage gap (disparity between mean wages for different demographic groups) between those with and those without a degree has risen to 83% (source D). Clearly, a college degree affords you an advantage worth its price.

America is a nation where parents work to afford their children every advantage, to build a better life. It is why immigrants dream of their children being doctors and lawyers, and why education has always been a central tenet of the American Dream. Because a college degree gives students a well-rounded education and life experience not afforded elsewhere, a competitive edge for employment, and opportunity to earn higher wages. The price may be high, but the reward is higher, making a college education well worth its cost.

What score would you give it? _____

Synthesis Essay #2

Many cultures have rituals to honor the dead, Native American tribes would often worship their ancestors, Ghanaians are buried in proverbial coffins that represent their qualities in life, etc. These memorials are an attempt to cope with the death of loved ones, however, other memorials, like the Holocaust Memorial Museum or some American landmarks are inaccurate and a waste of money. Those memorials wipe away the wrongdoings and realities of the events, and place a clean sheet that hides what actually occurred.

The Holocaust museum in the National Mall, Washing DC serves as a memorial to the millions of Jewish people that were slaughtered in the events of World War Two (Musser), but it presents a glaring inaccuracy: that the U.S. cared about the Jewish lives lost in the war. In the modern day almost all Americans recognize that the Holocaust was a tragedy, but that is not reflected in our countries actions at the time. The U.S. shunned and refused to help Jewish passengers on a ship who sailed to Florida seeking asylum, and that resulted in the slaughter of many of those people. It is disingenuous to purport that the United States was some kind of compassionate ally to the Jewish people when in reality they were just another bystander who did not want to help the Jewish people. Another example of these deceptions can be seen in the Monument of Christopher Columbus in Riverside Park, Easton, Pennsylvania (photo). The statue depicts a dashing man posing while looking upwards to the sky, yet that man was actually a psychopathic murderer and racist who subjugated thousands of Native Americans. Not only is the heroic depiction wrong, the features he is shown to have are wrong as well. There is no painting in existence of Christopher Columbus, so any statue made of a courageous man is not only depicting a murderer as such it is also just a guess of what he may have looked like.

Memorials are a needlessly expensive activity, with some large memorials taking of large portions of land and lots of money. These expensive memorials are often done with the premise of showing support to the people who are depicted, but as a Kelly Looking Horse, a Sioux Indian, described it "... [there are] better ways to help [American] Indians than building a big statue" (Downes). Any money that went to building a statue commemorating the deaths of Native Americans could have instead been donated to helping them, which could have a measurable impact instead of just making the artists feel good for "helping." Memorials do not reverse the past wrongs done to a people, no matter how much land or money is put into it, instead they may have a negative effect on the land. This can be seen with large memorials such Mount Rushmore, which required nearly 1 million dollars, or 14.4 million adjusted for inflation, along with the defacing of natural land.

Memorials are commonplace yet are inaccurate and wasteful, and are simply an attempt to reconcile the death of a loved one. Money spent on a memorial could go to something more substantial and accurate.

What score would you give it? _____

Synthesis Essay #3

Hollywood has a long-running history of films in the massive adventure genre, including adventures through the vastness of space. Although largely exaggerated for plot, these movies effectively highlight how little we understand about outer space and predict the boundless discoveries and life forms waiting to be encountered. But what blockbuster films excel in presenting space exploration as a goldmine of information waiting to be excavated, it lacks in depicting the well-known costs and dangers that governments and space agencies need to juggle before sending shuttles beyond the atmosphere. How much we can profit from business depends on how much we spend in construction; how much we learn about other planets depends on how far we damage the ecosystem in the process. It is imperative that we avoid hasty decisions and evaluate total costs and environmental impacts of space exploration before we let promising economic payout or increased knowledge lead us blindly towards danger.

Nothing in our modern society can function without monetary means to back it up, and space exploration is no exception. When Margaret R. McLean, on behalf of the Markkula Center for Applied Ethics, reports that "almost $7 billion will fly into NASA's coffers with around $5.3 billion dedicated to space exploration," Americans can reasonably be praying that the government has a 50% off coupon on that item (Source E); they fear that such a large sum is being taken away from services like healthcare and put into a project they will never see the outcome of. Andrew Chamberlain of The Tax Foundation, however, quells this fear with the fact that for every taxpayer dollar spent, only 6 cents goes into a category of 11 different functions in which space an technology is included (Source C). His data takes the billions that originally towered over our wallets and reduced it to a fraction of 6 cents; this shows that space exploration at the federal spending level will have little significant impact on the expenditures toward health and Medicare that receive the proportional 10 and 13 cents, respectively (Source C). But beyond the national capability alone, people want to see how space exploration could affect their individual economic lives. David Livingston provides a possible answer, pointing out how "the money that is spent" in the creation of shuttles, launch pads like the one in photo B, and control centers "goes to manufacturing, research and development, salaries, benefits, insurance companies" and plenty more (Source A and B). As each element comes together to send a team into space, such a wide range of business can flourish from the original federal investment, which can lead to economic benefits for people of all tax brackets. Space exploration is like an investment: you have to have a starting amount to put into play, but with careful management, one can expect a hearty return.

On top of economic management, space exploration demands that we show concern towards what our actions can do to extraterrestrial environments. Before even considering present possibilities, ethics investigators like McLean point to our destructive past on earth that has resulted in "the disruption of migratory routes, soil erosion, and species extinction" (Source E); if these outcomes are any indication of what may come from space exploration as we learn about potential benefits of moon soil on farming, we can only expect to see the devastation of galactic ecosystems that may easily affect life beyond the host planet. One could propose that we limit all space exploration to solely knowledge-seeking endeavors to thereby obviate any potential for ecological exploitation. But even if we lead with our best intentions, there's no guarantee we won't bring a foreign disease or microbe back to Earth, something Richard Greenberg in the journal American Scientist recounts lead the crews from the first moon landings to be "quarantined to prevent 'back contamination,' the hazard that some…germ might be riding with them" (Source F). Even past explorers have worried about the unknown; that one wrong move could cause the decimation of a population, alien or human, analogous to the vanishing of Native American populations by smallpox. We cannot assume that space exploration will not cause with it the alteration of the universe for the worse.

A lot of money and ecosystems are on the line as we push forward with space exploration. The issues of how much must be spent or how much will we harm should not, however, exist as a blockade to further advancement in space knowledge. The challenge becomes, rather, to develop the best technology with the least environmental impact, as our effectiveness in planning can determine how fast we learn about what, or who, is in the galaxy next door.

What score would you give it? _____

Scores

Synthesis Essay #1 - score 7, 8

Synthesis Essay #2 - score 7

Synthesis Essay #3 - score 7, 8

A WORD ON ARGUMENTATION

Argumentative essays aren't a novelty; there's little insight to add to the wealth of explanations on the subject. However, here are some fresh ways to think about it:

- The Argument essay **must be written like the Rhetorical Analysis text** was written, with persuasive and compelling arguments, layered with effective strategies and with a nuanced purpose. In short, that wonderfully complex Rhetorical speech or article you analyzed and concluded was highly effective, may just become the model for your own essay. You are the Rhetorical writer.

- **Good Argumentative essays are not simple**. Readers always assume they are simple because they are clear, organized, easy to follow and they make a lot of sense. Of course, they are; the easier to understand, the better the argument. But simple arguments often come from sophisticated thinking.

- **Do the thinking before the writing**. Often, Argumentative essays have a way of making sense as they continue and they make the most sense at the end. This happens because the writer was thinking his/her ideas through, while composing. It's best to think through those ideas before writing them, so that readers don't have to wait until the end of the argument to understand it fully. They may not be that patient or forgiving.

- **You're not arguing fact. You're not arguing Truth. You're arguing "my opinion makes sense."** The Argumentative essay is a well-argued, strongly presented, carefully crafted opinion. Call it anything you want, but it's still an opinion. You may not realize it, but calling it an opinion is liberating. Knowing that your argument doesn't have to be the truth of the universe feels like another day in the office, and this will very likely result in organic, thoughtful, genuine arguments. And that will make your essay more appealing.

The argumentation essay should really be called a **persuasive** essay, simply because "argumentative" sounds more aggressive than what this essay actually calls for. Being persuasive calls for the finesse of reasonable claims that account for small concessions, not the (sometimes) incendiary series of claims that (usually) permeate in argumentative essays.

The argument prompts vary from: short **statements**, an **excerpt** from a text, or a **situation**, all followed by a sub-related question or statement, that guides the reader's focus. You can respond in many ways, but the most common include: **agreeing** with the prompt's claim, **disagreeing** or **qualifying** the claim.

Common Problems in Arguments

Saying Nothing in Four Sentences

"Plato's *Allegory of the Cave* is one of times greatest philosophical ideas. Plato makes reality seem unlike reality with his Allegory of the Cave. Challenging reality itself is no easy task, many will shoot down this idea. Plato has a very viable view on how reality could be fake. One of the greatest philosophers known today gives people a different perception on what is real."

Big problem: opinionated claims without substance.

Making Claims that Don't Settle Anything

"A large number of the U.S. population are immigrants and with that comes a unique experience. They are left to question which culture they associate themselves with more. Their homeland or their new home? Although some would say cultural identity is not as important as one's sense of individuality, nationality is a basis for a person's individuality."

Big problem: is the essay about cultural identity, nationality, individuality? What's the stance?

Thinking that Claims can Substantiate Other Claims

Truman was a slave. Truman from the movie The Truman Show, represents those in bondage and slavery. Truman was obviously a slave; he was used for entertainment purposes. Truman was held against his will. He truly owned nothing, and most of the viewers did not care about Truman. The character Truman was an unwilling and unknowing slave.

Big problem: no rationale provided for claims made.

READING THE PROMPT

Much like in any of the other two essays, an effective reading of the prompt will increase the likelihood of an effective writing response. This is especially true of the Argument prompt; with an expressed goal of testing the student writer's ability to craft an argument, this prompt offers substantially less information on which to base a response, often a quotation or a philosophical tagline for which there is never a straight answer.

What the Argument Prompt Looks Like
AP ENGLISH LANGUAGE AND COMPOSITION SAMPLE
RESPONSE
Question 3
(Suggested time—40 minutes)

Context

This part of the prompt will provide information about the person who said "___" or the person who believed "___." Often, the prompt will also make clear in what framework the given quotation or idea is to be understood.

Text

Often a quotation or reference of some sort, this part presents a concept that will become the focus of your essay.

Task

This part is usually preceded by "write an essay in which…" and followed by a carefully worded assignment. Pay attention to it because that's what your essay will be about.

Breaking Down the Prompt

The keys to understanding the task of the prompt are **Terminology** and **Interpretation**.

To follow, here is a likely example of an Argument prompt, modeled after AP prompts.

Prompt Sample

This is an excerpt from an article on the relationship between place and the self.

> "Place, as a concept, refers to more than just the geographical (physical). The material location where people dwell, along with its visual characteristics and features: mountains, rivers, forests, etc. have an impact on those living in those places, because people share some form of connection to their surrounding environment. Every connection implies relation, which implies identification, which implies meaning. So, living somewhere always means something to those living there - something more."

In a well written essay, argue to the extent to which the article's claim that geographical location ("place") helps shape someone's identity is valid.

Terminology
Pay attention to the words used in the prompt above. In it, the words "place," and "identity" are begging for definition. Don't consider what you think it means. Forget about what you think, for now. What does the text say it means?

Interpretation
Consider the task's interpretation of these key terms. The task contextualizes the idea of "place," singularly as geographical, calling it a location so that the student-reader does not connote the word differently. It also implies that "place shapes identity," leaving the student-writer to consider, "to what extent."

What to do

- **Think** about the prompt long before you start writing. Thinking may mean: jotting down **clusters** of ideas, exploring concepts in short paragraphs of **free writing**, or simply staring at your pencil. Any of these is fine. Just don't jump into the writing before giving the prompt some thought.

- Pick one opinion and don't deviate from it. Every AP student-writer I've taught has had the same problem with the argument prompt; too many opinions. After reading the prompt, they agree, they disagree, they somewhat agree or somewhat disagree. They find every one of their opinions equally valid and can't decide which to argue. And it shows in their writing. Just don't pick "the right answer," just pick something you can argue comfortably for a page and a half.

READING THE TEXT

When reading the Argument prompt, remember that the texts vary between excerpts, statements or quotations that are often controversial and almost always welcoming of divergent opinions, for which there is never a straight yes or no answer.

Not unlike Rhetorical and Synthesis, this prompt demands three things: **read** the text, **paraphrase** the text for understanding, and **relate** that paraphrasing to the way the prompt interprets the text. The difference is that these three happen almost simultaneously as you read the Argumentative prompt.

Again, the prompt presents **an excerpt from an article**:

> "Place, as a concept, refers to more than just the geographical (physical). The material location where people dwell, along with its visual characteristics and features: mountains, rivers, forests, etc. have an impact on those living in those places, because people share some form of connection to their surrounding environment. Every connection implies relation, which implies identification, which implies meaning. So, living somewhere always means something to those living there."

And then, it tells you to, "argue to the extent to which the article's claim that geographical location ("place") helps shape someone's identity is valid."

What to do

1. Consider **your own response** to the text. What parts of the text lead you to interpret it one way or another?

2. **Relate your understanding** of the text to the direction outlined by the task in the prompt: "significance of 'place' in shaping someone's identity."

3. Reconcile the two and reason **how the prompt arrived at its conclusion.**

The Text is not the Task

The text provided by the Argument prompt (be it a quotation or a general, philosophical claim) **is not the task** the student-writer is supposed to write about. Not entirely. The quote may say something about "disobedience." The philosophical claim may say something about "identity." But the task attached to either one is the "real" concern of the prompt. While the quote may say that "disobedience is good," the task may be asking **whether that quote has relevance or value for today's society**. While the philosophical claim may say that "personal identity is more important than group identity," the task may ask to take a position on the relationship between the two. **The task always clarifies what course of action to take with the text provided**, so pay attention to the task. The text is always general enough to encourage any idea in response; just make sure to align your preferred response with what the task is asking.

The Text is not the Point

If the prompt presents a quote or idea that claims, "to belong is to understand why you belong," don't fixate your writing on the quote. **The text always presents an opportunity to go beyond it** - think about what belonging means, consider even that the quote may not be of merit, or may need rephrasing. Just don't get stuck on the text.

WRITING THE ESSAY

The Argumentative essay is composed in answer to three questions: **What, How** and **Why**. Respectively, the introduction answers the WHAT, the body answers the HOW and the conclusion answers the WHY. However, each section (Intro, Body, Conclusion) is also broken down in their respective questions.

In the **Introduction**, the three questions repeat themselves

- What are we talking about (**Topic**)?
- How is that relevant or important (**Context**)?
- Why do you think this way or that way about it (**Thesis**)?

The **thesis of the introduction** is further subdivided into these three

- What is your point (**Claim**)?
- How is that true (Evidence/**Support**)?
- Why does it matter or have significance (**Rationale**/Warrant)?

In the **Body**, these questions become:

- What is your **support** for the claim made in the thesis?
- How is that **true**, important, relevant, verifiable?
- Why does it say something significant about your **thesis**?

In some cases, the **How of the Body** can be divided into these questions as well

- What is your **evidence** (Quote/Example)?

- <u>How</u> does that **evidence support** your **claim** (Explain Example)?

- <u>Why</u> is the **evidence** crucial to the understanding of your **claim**?

In the **Conclusion**, these questions can take this form

- <u>What</u> fresh language can you use to **summarize** what we've been talking about?

- <u>How</u> can you connect that summary to something beyond this essay - to something **real and relatable**?

- <u>Why</u> have I been reading your essay this entire time? (and your reason had better be good)

INTRODUCTION

Good essays have great introductions. Great introductions are written after the essay is complete, when you have the luxury of knowing what it is you've been trying to say. And great introductory sentences are not rarely and almost always written last, because your first thought should anticipate your final thought.

Opening Sentence Tips:

   1. The opening sentence is very important because it affects the reader's disposition toward the essay. Make a good first impression.

   2. Don't write **empty openings**. Here are some types of empty openings:

     a. An opening that has **no relation to the rest of the essay**.

     The following essay on safety and freedom addresses the prompt's use of Mencken's quotation but does not bring him up again throughout the essay.

     "Mencken's observation that 'The average man does not want to be free. He simply wants to be safe' encompasses contemporary society's desire to place safety over freedom."

     b. Simply **rearranging the prompt**.

     The following essay on disobedience repeats an observation offered by the prompt.

     "Disobedience is a natural action one makes—it is bound to happen at some point."

     c. Sentences that sound **formulaic**, or include **clichés**.

This essay on freedom and safety presents an intro sentence that is too broad, has no clear stance and settles nothing.

"The balance between freedom and safety is one found in many situations today as well as those in the past."

3. Don't talk about something in the introduction that will not come up during the essay. Almost every element of the intro should **anticipate the content of the essay.**

4. While not the ultimate opening, some writers choose to begin with **the claim of their thesis** and dedicate the rest of the intro to substantiating it.

5. Using a **quotation from the text** is an acceptable way to begin answering the prompt, but it may limit the student-writer's originality and creativity.

1st Sentence

One way to Anticipate the thesis (and the rest of your essay) is accomplished by introducing the topic of your essay.

Topical Opening
Establish the <u>topic</u> (or general focus) of the essay by addressing the term employed in the prompt.

Example
"Historically, humor has been used to mock society's hardships and difficulties, to lessen the severity of a situation, and to lighten the mood; yet, these comedic productions often allude to much larger issues that can't be deliberately addressed by politicians or journalists because of societal norms, and the sensitivity of society towards certain topics of conversation." **(Score 8)**

Rationale
Topical introductory sentences allow for a focused control of the essay's direction, and it makes for a smooth transition from the topical opening sentence (say, on disobedience) to the closing thesis sentence (say, disobedience affords us personal growth through experience).

More Examples
"Disobedience is a natural action one makes—it is bound to happen at some point. But it is through disobedience that one grows, learning from mistakes, and blooming into a better person than before." **(Possible Score 4, 5)**

"Human beings are defined and shaped by an amalgamation of interplaying factors that are invisible to the human eye. One such factor is the ability to communicate with others through polite and pleasant speech in order to create and maintain relationships." **(Possible Score 8, 9)**

2nd – 3rd Sentence

Explain the issue
Narrow the general topic to a specific concern and establish your stance on the issue.

Example
"So, humorists use the lighthearted aspect of their work to merge the gap between the discussion of contentious issue and the (often) unexpressed polemic public opinion." **(Score 8)**

Rationale
These middle sentences make it easier to specify your essay's concern. For instance, the intro sentence on "polite speech" takes shape into "empty gestures," allowing the student-writer to present a thesis in the next sentence that would speak of polite speech as a meaningless facility of language, and a necessity of civilized societies.

More Examples
"This is true for all types of disobedience, from the broadest of concepts including political rebellions to relatively minute disobedience at home. Disobedience represents our human will to change" **(Possible Score 7, 8)**

"These catch phrases, such as "How are you", and "Nice to meet you" paradoxically convey a sense of care and curiosity towards the person receiving the expression, while being nothing more than an empty gesture." **(Possible Score 6, 7)**

"The evolutionary requirements for human progress have changed, survival is no longer sufficient, humankind actively seeks life, liberty, and happiness. However, as evidenced by Maslow's hierarchy of needs and the rationality of the human mind, people must meet basic needs, such as safety, before pursuing these commodities." **(Possible Score 8)**

Last Sentence

Thesis
Present a Claim, Evidence that supports it and the Rationale that explains it.

Example
"...their role is essential to social progress and advancements, as seen in political cartoons, that satirize a situation to highlight its flaws, and talk show hosts, that have the ability to deliver unfiltered news, and provide a more accurate representation of the issue." **(Score 8)**

Rationale
The thesis statement is the most important part of the introduction and should contain the elements listed above: claim, evidence, rationale. The first states what your stance is on the topic of discussion, the second explains how your stance can be proven true and the last explains why your explanations prove the claim you provided.

More Examples
"History has proven that safety has been prioritized over freedom and vice versa, these prioritizations are apparent in today's society more than ever." **(Possible Score 6)**

"Whether it be leaving your home country in a crisis, or facing an event leading to stricter policies, if it means being safer than it is prioritized." **(Possible Score 7, 8)**

Complete Introduction Example

Historically, humor has been used to mock society's hardships and difficulties, to lessen the severity of a situation, and to lighten the mood; yet, these comedic productions often allude to much larger issues that can't be deliberately addressed by politicians or journalists because of societal norms, and the sensitivity of society towards certain topics of conversation. So, humorists use the lighthearted aspect of their work to merge the gap between the discussion of contentious issue and the (often) unexpressed polemic public opinion. Their role is essential to social progress and advancements, as seen in political cartoons, that satirize a situation to highlight its flaws, and talk show hosts, that have the ability to deliver unfiltered news, and provide a more accurate representation of the issue.

(Score 8)

Introduction Examples

on

Safety vs. Freedom

Example A

Throughout history, mankind has worked to protect the things he holds most dear. Those are his family, his being, and his personal freedoms, established by nature's blessing for all living creatures. He cannot work towards protecting these things without their safety being secured first, for without safety, man cannot develop the basic foundation of contemporary society. Without safety he cannot develop systems of government, nor ideas to challenge these governments and established social orders.

(Possible Score 7,8)

Example B

Over the last millennium, the evolution of governments from empires and monarchies to democracies and republics reflects a growing human desire to be free. This development has engendered a philosophical debate over the balance between freedom and safety, with citizens desiring both personal liberties and individual protection. However, the two are inversely related, as when a government becomes more protective of its citizens, it often becomes more oppressive and restrictive of freedoms. While both freedom and safety are essential to a successful society, the human spirit has evolved to value freedom more and will often pursue freedom at the cost of safety. **(Score 9)**

Example C

In a contemporary society, it is evident that the assurance of safety comes with the restriction of some freedoms, such as free speech, independence, or having a choice over your actions. Yet, with knowledge of such, the average man would agree that safety comes before personal freedoms; and would gladly give up some rights if granted the promise of safety, especially in the essence of a tragic event. Whether it be leaving your home country in a crisis, or facing an event leading to stricter policies, if it means being safer than it is prioritized. **(Score 7)**

Example D

Years of people enjoying certain privileges can make the status quo feel like an entitlement. How can you strip me of something I've had since birth? This mentality is hard to change, but there is a type of evidence that can greatly reform the mindset of many: a national tragedy. The untimely loss of loved ones through acts of violence can make the entitlement a curse, one which a community desires to eradicate. When a community's welfare is jeopardized by some terroristic threat, victims are more willing to relinquish certain freedoms in order to prevent repetition and ensure peace of mind.

(Score 8)

BODY

The body paragraph often follows a specific pattern: the first part provides a claim, which guides the rest of the body discussion. This claim, often one sentence, answers the questions: WHAT are we going to talk about?

The body paragraph of an argumentative essay is indisputably the **most important part of the essay**. While Rhetorical intros are essential in establishing the purpose of the writing, as well as the rhetorical devices and strategies the writer successfully uses to convince his/her reader, the Synthesis and Argumentative body paragraphs are definitely essential in determining the AP reader's criticism of your essay. Synthesis bodies demand authentic engagement with the sources provided, but **Argumentative bodies** demand **creativity** and a **range** of examples. In arguments, the examples your reader wants, must have **depth** and **breadth**: an example that makes a superficial comparison between the rhetoric of your essay and say, concept A, will signal to the reader that you can make connections between ideas, but you cannot understand the significance of their connection. Similarly, examples that are too closely related, while readily providing immediate cohesion to your essay, demonstrate your inability to corelate ideas that are not clearly related. So, provide examples in your body paragraphs that demonstrate a **comprehensive** and **nuanced** understanding of a sophisticated idea.

What are Examples?

Argumentative body paragraph **examples** can make or break your essay. If your rhetoric is interesting but you are not using historical, political, social, psychological, or modern examples to illustrate your point, then your ideas will be judged as unsubstantiated. Examples should take your essay's rhetoric and **give it shape**, by molding it into an image or a concept the reader may be familiar with; after all, examples are representations of the concept you're trying to explain. Without examples, your essay's ideas are rooted in midair.

1st Sentence

Claim
This sentence seeks to justify the thesis, so use one of the reasons provided to clearly state your argument.

Example
"Cartoonists have the power to depict a social injustice in a hyperbolized way to emphasize the flaws that might not be apparent to all people." **(Possible Score 7, 8)**

Rationale
This sentence establishes a topical claim that will guide the rest of the body.

More Examples
"Polite speech is necessary in human culture because it reminds us that we are capable of being kind."
(Possible Score 7, 8)

"For those in grim situations often the choice is risk for freedom." **(Possible Score 4, 5)**

"Safety begets freedom, the knowledge that one is secure in their rights to explore the endless opportunity life has to offer increases motivation to socialize and explore."
(Possible Score 5, 6)

"One of the most alluring facets of America are the numerous freedoms of speech, religion, and other expressions, granted to its people and actively defended by courts on all levels of government." **(Possible Score 6, 7)**

Middle Sentences

Support

The middle sentences (addressing the aforementioned claim on competition) require the following things (at least 4 out of the 5)

Introduce Evidence

"This idea is prevalent to all throughout American history..."

State Evidence

"...like the political cartoon of a broken snake, with each piece labeled the abbreviations of the thirteen colonies, representing a divided nation that could not survive in the War of Independence without unity and cohesion."

Explain Evidence

"This underlying message had strong implications for the future of the United States, and was easily interpreted by the drawing of a broken snake; this image was a driving force in joining the American forces together, and could have been a factor in forming the nation that exists today."

Present And Explain More Evidence (if possible or necessary)

"Political cartoonists also convey ideas of social reform, as seen in the various cartoons drawn in the late 1800's (the Second Industrial Revolution), that displayed the cruelties and poor living condition of immigrants and factory workers in the United States, that had limited rights, under the monopolizing industries, like steel mills, owned and operated by a single person, Andrew Carnegie."

Relate Evidence to Thesis

"The cartoons exposed these hardships and sparked change, like the formation of worker's unions to protect their rights."

Connect Evidence to General Idea

"Such ideas could not have been directly explained, as those who spoke out would suffer harsher consequences than the humorists, showing the effectiveness of their work."

*Note: Argumentative essays must include (what some call) an **acknowledgement of the opposition**. This "nod" to the opposition should be written into the body paragraph. It is recommended to **NOT** dedicate **an entire paragraph** to the opposing view because it may either confuse the reader about your stance or weaken your argument in comparison. Preferably, the acknowledgement should **NOT** be written in the **beginning** or **closing sentences**. Instead, it is best to bury the acknowledgement somewhere in the **middle of the body** because having it in the beginning may give the impression your paragraph's argument will be in response to the opposition, which takes away from your independent argument, and having it at the end allows the opposition a final word; it's your essay, not theirs.

Body Examples

Example A
American citizens can protest and fight for their beliefs, and practice their religion freely, even if members of Congress and the executive branch disagree. In a stark contrast to the shining shores of liberty, many governments around the world oppress opinions and practices that clash with their beliefs, punishing innocent people for simply believing in differing thoughts. This deprivation of freedom creates a dangerous environment where nonconformists are punished with imprisonment, public beatings, and sometimes, death.

(Possible Score 5, 6)

Biggest problem: lacks specific example.

Example B
Besides a warm lunch, crates of crayons and markers, and God's grace in the form of an hour recess, schools have always made it a focal point to ensure the safety of their student body. But the parents of 17 young adults had no way of knowing they would drop off their students into their graves, on Valentine's day of all days. A day coveted for love became one of lives cut short by a mentally disturbed school shooter murdering his former peers at Marjory Stoneman Douglas high school in Parkland, Florida. The door-holder was now the door-checker, asking for the password to open the perpetually locked doors of all schools in South Florida. Kids petitioning for better school food became the ones left behind at congress's door begging for gun control laws to pass. Our children, our friends, lost their lives because tips suggesting the danger of this criminal were disregarded, because assault weapons were so pervasive to even young

individuals, and because mental illness is often dismissed or joked about. In the wake of such a tragedy, Americans of all ages pushed for raising the age to own an assault rifle and explanations and greater action from our polices force, which a day earlier were absent from major news outlets. People became willing - desperate - to limit gun ownership and heighten school security after valentine day because they needed some justice for the loss of 17 innocent souls.

(Score 9)

Greatest Strengths: vivid examples, provocative language, and clear focus, to name a few.

Example C

This is seen in dystopian novels such as Lois Lowry's The Giver. The government of Lowry's society has eliminated all forms of suffering and hardship by assigning jobs, dictating marriage partners, and transferring all painful memories to a single citizen known as the Receiver. Through this, they hoped to create a harmonious and egalitarian state where discrimination, prejudice, and pain are unknown. However, by imposing such control, they are depriving their citizens of their basic human rights and independence. In the end, the protagonist escapes the strictures of his society in order to pursue a life of freedom, despite the inevitable pain that he will endure. Imagine if in today's world, a government attempted to deprive its people of a freedom as basic as memory. This regime would immediately be subject to intense diplomatic outrage as well as a popular revolt from its citizens, protesting their blatant disregard for universal liberties. **(Possible Score 4, 5)**

Biggest problem: although an attempt is made to connect the fictional example to a real setting, not "real" circumstance is addressed, and the fictionality of the example makes the point lose validity because the issue discussed is a real issue, while the example isn't.

Last Sentence

Insight
The evidence, interlaced with analysis, has been leading up to a complete analysis (or understanding), usually expressed in the last sentence.

Examples
"Such ideas could not have been directly explained, as those who spoke out would suffer harsher consequences than the humorists, showing the effectiveness of their work."
(Possible Score 8)

"This demonstrates contemporary prioritization of freedom, even at the cost of welfare." **(Possible Score 4)**

"Migrants from both Syria and Myanmar demonstrate the basic human need for freedom and the endless efforts people will go to obtain it." **(Possible Score 6, 7)**

"Perseverance played a key role in the Native American thought process, in which human tendency is intrinsic to self-sustainability." **(Possible Score 5, 6)**

Complete Body Example

Cartoonists have the power to depict a social injustice in a hyperbolized way to emphasize the flaws that might not be apparent to all people. This idea is prevalent to all throughout American history, like the political cartoon of a broken snake, with each piece labeled the abbreviations of the thirteen colonies, representing a divided nation that could not survive in the War of Independence without unity and cohesion. This underlying message had strong implications for the future of the United States, and was easily interpreted by the drawing of a broken snake; this image was a driving force in joining the American forces together, and could have been a factor in forming the nation that exists today. Political cartoonists also convey ideas of social reform, as seen in the various cartoons drawn in the late 1800's (the Second Industrial Revolution), that displayed the cruelties and poor living condition of immigrants and factory workers in the United States, that had limited rights, under the monopolizing industries, like steel mills, owned and operated by a single person, Andrew Carnegie. The cartoons exposed these hardships and sparked change, like the formation of worker's unions to protect their rights. Such ideas could not have been directly explained, as those who spoke out would suffer harsher consequences than the humorists, showing the effectiveness of their work.

(Possible Score 9)

Body Example Explained

BAD Paragraph Example

The actions of radical individuals who oppose the existing government have also proven to be influential in the progression of society. Figures such as Martin Luther King Jr., Malcolm X, or Mahatma Gandhi have all proven to have the ability to change society for the better by rebelling and organizing social movements. These individuals represent the disobedient individuals who have made great change in society for the rest of civilization. They are rebels who see an issue in society or the government and recognize the need for change and progress. By striving for change and progress, the individuals have inspired movements of civil disobedience that inspire change in society to make the world a better place for all of mankind and improve the rights and bring equality to all people. **(Possible Score 4)**

Analysis

- This paragraph **sets the focus** in the first sentence: "radical individuals…influential"

- While the paragraph presents **possible examples** in the second sentence: "Martin Luther King, Gandhi," it fails to substantiate them.

- The next two sentences are **chatty,** and offer no explanations as to why these figures were chosen as example to support the Body's claim.

- The **insight** provided in the last sentence is **empty** because it **not tethered to any specific example.**

BETTER Paragraph Example

The actions of radical individuals who oppose the existing government have also proven to be influential in society's progress. Figures such as Martin Luther King Jr. and Mahatma Gandhi have proven to have the ability to change society for the better by rebelling and organizing social movements. <u>In the year 1963, Martin Luther King Jr. led a march of over 250,000 people in hopes of gaining freedom and rights. In 1893 Mahatma Gandhi refused to comply with the racial rules that the Indian government enforced thereby starting his life of civil disobedience towards the oppressive forces in the world, particularly the Indian government.</u> By striving for change and progress, the individuals have inspired movements of civil disobedience that inspire change in society to make the world a better place for all of mankind and improve the rights and bring equality to all people.

(Possible score 6, 7)

Analysis

- Adding the **specific examples** about King and Gandhi (see underlined section) **fix** the central **problem** of the paragraph.

- Also, removing Malcolm X from the paragraph (see Bad Example) **narrows the focus** to similar movements (King and Gandhi).

- The insight at the end is stronger now, because of the **specific details** about King and Gandhi, but still has a fluffy, "better place for all mankind," kind of empty commentary.

CONCLUSION

There are (really) only two things that matter in a conclusion:

- **First**, <u>reflect on your thesis</u>. The first time your thesis enters the essay is in the introduction and it has something to prove, so it's assertive and demanding. When your thesis leaves the essay, it should sound **reflective and contemplative**, with nothing left to prove.

- **Last**, <u>ponder on the profound ramifications of your argument</u>. If your argument were a tree: the fruit would be the thesis (fully formed), the branches would be your reasons (supporting and bearing the fruit) and the roots would be the many premises on which your tree stands – the very thing that gives your argument meaning, importance, life. That's your conclusion.

Simple Outline

W – Wrap it up. Synthesize. Condense. Begin the ending. While this sentence can echo earlier ideas, it should not repeat earlier sentences. Here's a tip: look at the first sentence of each body paragraph, distill its most important ideas and connect them in this sentence.

E – Escape the essay. The reader wants to know you can think beyond the prompt, that you can see the real-life connections (and implications) of the topic you've been discussing. Here's a tip: create an extended analogy that allows for thematic mobility from the topic you've been discussing, to a topic familiar to the reader.

B – Big Meaning: Say something significant, impactful, something worth remembering. Just like first impressions, the last sentence should leave a mark on the reader. Here's a tip:

save whatever (attractive) claim-based sentence you think of during the composition of your essay for the very end. Save the best for last.

Example A
"Humorists have a versatile role that enables them to articulate ideas that might be socially unacceptable in other job positions. Both political and social reforms have been substantiated because of the role they play, and provide a loophole to discussing difficult topics. In a highly polarized world, humor is an important outlet for society."
(Possible Score 7, 8)

Example B
"Humans care more about safety than they do personal freedom, because it is impossible to have the latter without the first. How can one feel free if they do not first feel safe? If one spends their life afraid and hiding from others, then are they truly free despite being given complete freedom on paper? People need rules and regulations from their government to keep them safe and guarantee their protection, which is rightfully placed at a higher regard than freedom."
(Possible Score 6, 7)

Example C
"Polite speech is a valuable mechanism that provides for the integration of individuals into society and for their overall well-being. But more than a mechanism, it is a virtue, for only by having consideration and showing kindness towards others, can the human race continue its existence as a social creature. **(Possible Score 8)**

Example D
"When freedoms allow people to freely slaughter others and target our loved ones, we will readily pay to restrict these "freedoms" and secure our own safety in the future. No sane individual would want these tragedies to occur, but the best

thing we as a community can do moving past them is adjusting laws to prevent a repeated offense. Our goal shouldn't be to simply adjust after a tragedy; rather, we should actively assess laws to prevent the first offense."

(Possible Score 8, 9)

PACING THE ESSAY
(40 mins.)

10 Minutes
(The Text)

    1. Read the text provided (quotation, excerpt, etc.) **several times**, each time examining its possible meaning.

    2. Consider the many ramifications of the text, as the text is often an invitation for discourse on the issue presented.

(The Task)

    1. The text is not the task. The prompt identifies its own task. So **focus on the task**, usually presented at the end of the prompt.

    2. Recognize the **key words** of the task, words that imply a specific reading of the text.

25 Minutes
(The Essay)

    1. Write out your thesis, chances are that your introduction will flow out it. The thesis should turn the task of the prompt into a claim and use your own examples as your support.

    2. Choose examples that are historical, anecdotal, etc.; **hypothetical examples usually lead to chatty essays**.

5 minutes
(The revision)

    1. Proofread your essay, looking for grammatical mistakes, or phrases that are nonsensical to ensure a clean essay, with strong ideas. **Fix what you can.**

Complete Argumentation Essay Examples

This section includes a selection of Argumentation essays; each scored, like many of the paragraphs presented beforehand, ranging from mid to high. I decided not to include low-scoring essays because their glaring issues often make them easier to recognize. So I included essays that are neither all good nor all bad, instead, they are - each of them - good and bad, with laudable moments and page-tearing-what-were-you-thinking moments; not only does this varying quality makes them more challenging to score, but realistically, that is how essays are written, with good, bad, and ugly moments.

Essay #1

Laughter and cheer are the two weapons of the comedian, or at least the ones most familiar to us. Yet, to humor is to provoke, and humorists seem to have an impetus both permitting and encouraging them to wrestle controversy with an unadulterated wit that most politicians and public figures would dearly covet. And so, when Alain de Botton, an acclaimed author and documentary maker, implies that comedians can transcend societal biases and ethics, he is not only entirely correct, but he is broaching a serious issue in modern society, where sometimes the only manner to approach crisis, as existential as it may be, is through satire.

The "diplomatic immunity" that comedians possess is a dangerously powerful asset; a venue to question tyranny, incompetence, and corruption. Take for example the famous political cartoon of the captain leaving his ship, which illustrates Otto von Bismarck walking out of a war vessel with his hands in his pockets, the young Kaiser Wilhelm looking at him with stupid and self-assured eyes. This clever metaphor for the state of the German State encapsulates the author's views without having an argument be put forth to be dismantled and silenced by the empire, as many publications were. More importantly, this message reached all sectors of the German population, even Bismarck himself, who on his death bed states "it is a good one." It is fair to question the place of comedy now, however, as the rise of the German Empire is a far bit of time removed from us, but the matter remains the same. Dave Chapelle is a man who is known, admired, and respected for his social commentary and "radical" comedy, being one of the few people on television who has said the "forbidden word" coined by slavers, without receiving very much backlash. There is no other platform where this would be permitted, due to the dogged stubbornness and hypersensitivity of modern society, and yet Chapelle uses the infamous n-bomb along with other outrageous stereotypes and other minority groups. This is very much in line with Botton's philosophy, proving that comedians do often indeed "convey with impunity messages that might be dangerous or impossible to state directly." To those who would still differ, I ask you this: why is the White House Correspondence Dinner one of the most viewed and televised events in the country? Presidents from Nixon to Obama approached this particular event with a very lax and comedic attitude, and yet they have deeply woven their rhetoric and thoughts into them, something few people likely even noticed. Take Reagan saying "we are firing the missiles now" after a policy change to increase military funding during times of lessening Soviet tensions, or Obama playing the introduction of the Lion King after saying that video evidence of his birth was found, in reference to Donald Trump's viral claims of his illegitimacy as a natural born U.S. citizen. Politicians, when acting as humorists, can structure, defend, and attack arguments and discussions previously out of their reach, a testament to the power of comedy and the place of the humorist in society.

Ultimately, Botton's affirmation is, unsurprisingly, an affirmation. If Cicero moved men to action with humor, and Rockefeller's hegemony was challenged by political cartoonists, then who is to deny the humorist's power and place in the world?

(Score 9)

Essay #2

Years of people enjoying certain privileges can make the status quo feel like an entitlement. How can you strip me of something I've had since birth? This mentality is hard to change, but there is a type of evidence that can greatly reform the mindset of many: a national tragedy. The untimely loss of loved ones through acts of violence can make the entitlement a curse, one which a community desires to eradicate. When a community's welfare is jeopardized by some terroristic threat, victims are more willing to relinquish certain freedoms in order to prevent repetition and ensure peace of mind.

There was a time only 20 years ago when you could walk a family member to a plane's departure gate and watch them fly off as they smoke comfortably in the cabin. The airport environment was relaxed: no long metal detector lines; no restricted areas; peace. But all of a sudden 4 planes come crashing into the hearts of all Americans, watching in horror as terrorists hijack the aircrafts and destroy thousands of lives, a scenario which had never before occurred to us as a subject of major concern. After September 11, 2001, the first thing you encounter on your lengthy journey to board a plane is the TSA, which was set up to thoroughly check passengers and prevent weapons from being snuck onboard. Even beyond airports, the Patriot Act, which was passed without the scrutiny of many American citizens, allowed the NSA to monitor the internet with the intent of taking preemptive action against any potential extremist threats. If you told anyone before 9-11 that the government should place numerous checkpoints before boarding any form of transportation and that they need access to all of our search activity and website browsing, you'd be tried for treason against the land of the free. However, after seeing evil rain down from clear blue skies and kill over 3,000 of our nation's brothers and sisters, anything to "win" the unwillingly entered war on terrorism needed to be done. So if one must wait 2 hours to go through customs, the average American wouldn't give it a second thought, because this means something is being put in place to keep our airways safe.

School is an institution where young minds are cultivated and the capable youth become the future of our nation. Besides a warm lunch, crates of crayons and markers, and God's grace in the form of an hour recess, schools have always made it a focal point to ensure the safety of their student body. But the parents of 17 young adults had no way of knowing they would drop off their students into their grave, on Valentine's day of all days. A day coveted for love became one of lives cut short by a mentally disturbed school shooter murdering his former peers at Marjory Stoneman Douglas high school in Parkland, Florida. The door-holder was now the door-checker, asking for the password to open the perpetually locked doors of all schools in South Florida. Kids petitioning for better school food became the ones left behind at congress's door begging for gun control laws to pass. Our children, our friends, lost their lives because tips suggesting the danger of this criminal were disregarded, because assault weapons were so pervasive to even young individuals, and because mental illness is often dismissed or joked about. In the wake of such a tragedy, Americans of all ages pushed for raising the age to own an assault rifle and explanations and greater action from our polices force, which a day earlier were absent from major news outlets. People became willing- desperate- to limit gun ownership and heighten school security after valentine day because they needed some justice for the loss of 17 innocent souls. Everyone was willing to give up the freedom of relaxed rules and regulations because we wanted the freedom of being buried by our kids, not burying them.

When freedoms allow people to freely slaughter others and target our loved ones, we will readily pay to restrict these "freedoms" and secure our own safety in the future. No sane individual would want these tragedies to occur, but the best thing we as a community can do moving past them is adjusting laws to prevent a repeated offense. Our goal shouldn't be to simply adjust after a tragedy; rather, we should actively assess laws to prevent the first offense.

(Score 8)

Essay #3

All progress in a society is based upon a universal, innate desire to live beyond survival. The evolutionary requirements for human progress have changed, survival is no longer sufficient, humankind actively seeks life, liberty, and happiness. However, as evidenced by Maslow's hierarchy of needs and the rationality of the humankind, people must meet basic needs, such as safety, before pursuing these commodities. Therefore, the average individual desires to be both safe and free, but must be safe to then pursue an active and meaningful freedom.

Individuals are innately motivated to achieve certain needs in a certain order. This is best exemplified by Maslow's hierarchy of needs, which states that individuals must meet lower level needs before progressing to higher level needs. In this hierarchy, physiological needs are the first priority and self-actualization is the ultimate goal of existence. Furthermore, in between these extremities lies safety and the societal needs granted by freedom. From Maslow's hierarchy of needs, one can discern that human beings must first achieve safety to then shift their attention to achieving freedom and the esteem and cognitive needs it provides.

Humans are rational and sentient beings; they are able to reason and feel. As rational beings, we naturally seek to understand the surrounding world to then attribute meaning to it. As sentient beings, we engage in actions that produce pleasure and avoid those that end in pain to ensure survival. When these rational and sentient facets are combined, the result is the human mind. The human mind's sentience commands survival through instincts, making survival one of the primary objectives of life. But the mind's rational aspect craves more, it finds that survival alone is a primitive aim, instead it seeks to use its rational faculty to purse an independent course, to purse freedom. The freedom of thought endowed to us by our rationality naturally expresses itself in freedom of action. Retrospectively, the mind's sentience precedes its rationality, hence human beings seeks freedom as a complement to survival, not as an alternative.

It is evident that individuals strive to enrich their lives through the pursuit of freedom. But with this freedom comes a price, responsibility. For the test of our progress, above all, will be what we have done with our freedom.

(Score 7, 8)

The Almost Adequate Essay

One of the most difficult essays, and one of my most commonly scored essays, is the **5/6 essay**. This is the essay that stands in the threshold of inadequate (4) and could've entered into adequate (6), but it isn't bad enough to be the former nor good enough to be the latter. These can be a challenge. The key is to remember what adequate essays read like:

6 Adequate
These essays **get the job done**: presenting a **clear thesis**, though **not** particularly **sophisticated**, and organizing **focused ideas** in developed paragraphs. However, they may only offer **sufficiently developed textual examples**, with less detailed and/or **less convincing, superficial explanations**. These essays provide more summary than necessary and often **replace insight with simple commentary**. Syntax and mechanics are often correct, with small indelicacies, but the verbs may be weak and the language, artless. Big problem: **lacks insight**.

Example (5/6)

It is inevitable that throughout history the acts of disobedience has led to the progress of social and political rights of the people. Being disobedient in the sense of disregarding the unethical beliefs or laws of the land to fight for a moving cause in the good of all men and women, so that eventually all can become treated with equal respect to their inalienable rights. Whether it be in the topic of education or suffrage, social movements and protests against the established authority have many times led to some sort of progress one step at a time.

In modern times we have seen endless issues regarding certain rights around the world, one important topic is of a women's right to education in which acts of rebellion and protest have shown impactful progress. In regions such as North Africa and the Middle East it is often frowned upon in Muslim cultures that a woman may seek out for education. A notable example of a sacrifice for this cause was when a 14 year old Muslim girl stood up for her right to an education and was shot in the face for trying to attend school in which she survived. This act of disobedience showed a courageous young lady making a stand for thousands if not millions of girls in those regions that wish to attend a school; and get an education for their future. The action did not go unnoticed millions of caring people around the world spread the news through social media and has helped build programs that help these young ladies further their knowledge in their right to a proper education. Without this brave instance of disobedience many will have not known about this issue and the progress on the social rights of education for women continue.

Another concerning issue that has been making progress through acts of protest and social movements against governments in foreign nations and even the United States has been immigration. It could be tracked down to the times of colonization where many immigrants from England that came to the New World were against the nation's policy on religion and social wellbeing amongst classes. They moved to the New World to make a stand to the government that their treatment was unbearable which would eventually lead to advancements in their religious tolerance and social equality. A rising problem regarding immigration, is the ban of certain refugees from countries such as Syria from entering the

United states as ordered by President Donald Trump through an executive order; where people are trying to escape their country because of a political concern, but then disregarded of their reasons being based on their ethnicity and religion from whence they came. In order to stop this executive order passed by President Trump many have gone to airports and disturbed civil peace and have protested against the elected President's decision which has a caused a movement worldwide of protestors in places such as Paris and London to unban the poor Refugees suffering in these impoverished, terrorized countries from entering The United States. This move towards progress has put a temporary stop as the federal courts have been deciding if it is constitutional. It was through the defiance of the powerful leader's decision that discrimination has been lessened and that they can hold their social rights and use the visas granted to them to enter the United States.

While it is the belief that disobedience is the root of an evil path it has shown that it can alleviate a great good in all of humanity. Bringing awareness to the social eye and spreading ethical beliefs to places worldwide. As the further history goes the more social issues get recycled from the fabrics of times and yet another disobedient act must take place stopping it from continuing. It is through the defiance of power that the people's rights will truly make progress turn away from those unfair and biased ideas.

Grading Practice

This section offers a selection of Argumentative essays for your review. These essay address different prompts (which should become clear in their respective theses), and contain moments with writing errors and indelicacies, as well as artful and articulate moments. Take into consideration everything you've learned from this part of the book and score the following essays, as best you can. Remember that these essays were written under "40 minutes" (as would be the case the day of the test), and so should be rewarded for what they do right, not so much penalized for what they do wrong. If an essay doesn't seem to fit one score, give it two; chances are that the essay exceeds the criteria for one score (say 5), but does not quite meet the criteria for a higher score (say 6). This can happen, but try your best to assign each essay a single score. After you score each one, you'll find an answer page with all the scores, following the essay pages.

Scoring Guidelines

9 Highly Effective
These essays have everything in the description of an 8, but show a nuanced understanding of a complex issue, demonstrate a facility to successfully persuade its audience and read with a noted sophistication of language.

8 Effective
These essays offer original insight and elaborate extensively, with creative introductions and meaningful conclusions, all the while using sophisticated language. They go beyond general commentary on the issue presented in the prompt, and they often use specific examples to substantiate the claims. Most importantly, these essays make compelling arguments that effectively demonstrate their understanding of the task in the prompt and its ramifications.

7 More than Adequate
These essays meet the criteria of a 6, but they offer more insight and more developed examples. The examples are better developed, with a notable amount of grace and refinement.

6 Adequate
These essays get the job done: presenting a clear thesis, though not particularly sophisticated, and organizing focused ideas in developed paragraphs. However, they may only offer sufficiently developed textual examples, with less detailed and/or less convincing superficial explanations. These essays provide more summary than necessary and often replaces insight with simple commentary. Syntax and mechanics are often correct, with small indelicacies, but the verbs may be weak and the language, artless. Big problem: lacks insight.

5 Almost Adequate
These essays are more than inadequate (4) but not impressive enough to earn a 6. The thesis contains minimal analysis, with an unspecified claim, the bodies feel like summaries with some commentary and examples that are not expanded on. These essays are just superficial. There is an attempt at organization: Intro, Body, Conclusion, but there are too many redundancies, vague verbs, and simple vocabulary.

4 Inadequate
These essays are unacceptable. There is no real thesis, just a restatement of the prompt, without valid or with weak evidence; the introductions don't offer any real direction for the rest of the essay. The body paragraphs basically summarize, offer little or no examples, with an immature reading or analysis of the prompt. Generally, these essays don't advance any ideas or settle any conversations; they're boring, unimaginative, and repetitive.

3-2 Little Success

Argumentative Essay #1

Since the beginning of humankind, we have been curious creatures, and it is through that curiosity that we have pushed boundaries and broken into new eras. Some of the world's greatest achievements have occurred because of measured disobedience, or the act of breaking rules for moral or political reasons. This has expanded and challenged social norms in a positive way for all of our history.

The act of measured disobedience in order to achieve social progress is prevalent in writing. An advocate for this was Oscar Wilde himself. Everything about him was controversial and very much unlike anyone else in his time period. In one of his most popular books, "The Picture of Dorian Gray," Wilde portrays the sin of indulgence by allowing his character complete freedom in his actions. The character was promiscuous and impulsive, which were qualities that were strongly frowned up in the 19th century, as well as in any century. But by writing about this man's unrestrained adventures, he was sending a message to the public that to be oneself is nothing to be ashamed of. That was pretty much his philosophy, and he spent his entire life being unapologetically himself. Whether it was by writing provocative novels or by being blatantly open and comfortable with his sexuality, to the point where he was even imprisoned for these things. He went against what it meant to be a respectable member of society and instead rebelled against standards he was expected to uphold.

Through a rational and controlled method of disobedience, society has been able to evolve from antiquated worldly views. An example of this is present in Thoreau's essay "Civil Disobedience," in which he talks about how sometimes it is necessary to break certain laws for moral reasons. During the time he wrote this, slavery was a widely accepted practice throughout the country. He pointed out his anti-slavery opinion and that sometimes it is necessary to go against the current and to disobey in times when it is done to defeat a greater evil. His goal in writing this was to get people to realize that they must not blindly follow the law. Citizens need to create their own opinions and thoughts and know when they must rebel against certain ideals.

In order for progress to be made, we need to break through mental barriers and be innovative and open-minded in the things we say and feel. It is not the job of the people to be complacent. It is our duty to grow and expand our minds and our beliefs by going against the things we know to be against our standard of beliefs or obsolete.

What score would you give it? _____

Argumentative Essay #2

Over the last millennium, the evolution of governments from empires and monarchies to democracies and republics reflects a growing human desire to be free. This development has engendered a philosophical debate over the balance between freedom and safety, with citizens desiring both personal liberties and individual protection. However, the two are inversely related, as when a government becomes more protective of its citizens, it often becomes more oppressive and restrictive of freedoms. While both freedom and safety are essential to a successful society, the human spirit has evolved to value freedom more and will often pursue freedom at the cost of safety.

Often, governments that oppress their citizens justify this exploitation by saying it is to ensure their citizens' safety. This is seen in dystopian novels such as Lois Lowry's The Giver. The government of Lowry's society has eliminated all forms of suffering and hardship by assigning jobs, dictating marriage partners, and transferring all painful memories to a single citizen known as the Receiver. Through this, they hoped to create a harmonious and egalitarian state where discrimination, prejudice, and pain are unknown. However, by imposing such control, they are depriving their citizens of their basic human rights and independence. In the end, the protagonist escapes the strictures of his society in order to pursue a life of freedom, despite the inevitable pain that he will endure. Imagine if in today's world, a government attempted to deprive its people of a freedom as basic as memory. This regime would immediately be subject to intense diplomatic outrage as well as a popular revolt from its citizens, protesting their blatant disregard for universal liberties. This demonstrates contemporary prioritization of freedom, even at the cost of welfare.

Throughout history, countless revolutions and insurrections have illustrated the lengths to which the masses will go to obtain freedom. In the eighteenth century, the American colonists were part of the largest and most powerful empire in the world, yet dared to risk their economic and sociopolitical security in order to gain sovereignty and detach themselves from British rule. Under the command of this European empire, the colonists enjoyed the substantial flow of food and resources as well as military protection from Native Americans and foreign powers. The British attempted to aid the colonies through the supply of goods and through the establishment of a few regulations but these ultimately ensued resentment and disdain from the colonists. Due to the enmity which developed from the excessive control from the European power, the Americans chose to forgo their benefits and assets, in addition to their physical safety, to fight for their freedom in the perilous battles of the American Revolution. This same aspiration is what drove the subsequent revolutions of France, Haiti, and Serbia, modeling the exemplary United States. This nation had set a precedent which shaped humans' innate pursuit of liberty over the convenience of security.

In addition to the extensive historical precedent, modern examples and current events detail the human preference of freedom of security. Across the world, religious, ethnic, and racial minorities are downtrodden and oppressed by authoritarian governments. Many members of these groups go to extraordinary lengths to escape this mistreatment and tyranny, fleeing their home countries to pursue freedom in a new land. For example, the plight of Syrian refugees escaping the political turmoil in the Middle East show the courage and resolve shown by those who crave liberty. They face precarious conditions at sea and an uncertain future in their adopted country, yet they risk these perils in order to pursue a better and freer life. Another example of this incredible bravery in the face of persecution is the Rohingya people, a primarily Muslim group in Myanmar, a Buddhist country, who have been historically oppressed for their religion and their practices. In recent years, they have fled, enduring arduous treks and hazardous voyages to escape persecution and find religious freedom. Migrants from both Syria and Myanmar demonstrate the basic human need for freedom and the endless efforts people will go to obtain it.

When looking past the surface of the discussion of one's disposition to freedom and safety, we can question whether one is ever truly either of these things. Do our decisions genuinely reflect our choice to be free or safe if no matter what, we are neither of these things? In a world of high-tech weapons and unpredictable leadership figures can we ever be "safe"? With strict laws and regulations which we are in compliance of and heavily monitored internet usage will we ever be 'free'? If we can never have either than what choice is there to be made?

What score would you give it? _____

Argumentative Essay #3

Disobedience is a natural action one makes—it is bound to happen at some point. But it is through disobedience that one grows, learning from their mistakes, and blooming into a better person than they were before. Most people would note that the most common age for disobedience to occur is at a young age, so by the time children are young adults, their perspective on situations and social interactions improve significantly. The concept of disobedience can only be fully understood when it is interpreted as the first step of a large learning process—life.

The necessity of disobedience as a human trait is represented through the ripple of events in one's life, when disobedience occurs starting from a very young age. It is when the five-year-old boy is told not to climb up the slide at the playground because he will fall and get hurt, but does it anyways and ends up falling. It is when the fifth-grade girl is instructed to not cheat on a test because she will be penalized for it, but does it anyways and ends up going to detention. It is because of these occurrences in one's life that people realize why disobeying could lead to a stronger human being, and a brighter future overall. After that, the little boy learned that not following the rules could lead to pain and suffering, and the little girl realized that being self-confident in herself leads to a greater outcome—all things obtained through the process of defying, and learning from it. In a way, disobedience is a virtue.

Lois Lowry's novel The Giver, encompasses the way a fictional character allows his individual ideals to illuminate the way he feels his life should be, fighting against the social norm in the utopian society he lives in. The government's strategies of maintaining "utopian" habits are by having its citizens follow a strict guideline on how one should live, causing every character who is aware of what is going on, feel like a prisoner seeking freedom. Although from birth the main character was raised through the standards of the community, it is through disobedience that this character succeeds in escaping the boundaries of the restricted area, and experiencing "Elsewhere." Through disobeying his society's standards, he is at a major advantage—having the ability to experience beyond the norm.

Irish author Oscar Wilde recognizes the fact that, "it is through disobedience, that progress [is] made." It is commonly known that people learn through their mistakes; they decipher right from wrong in doing this. By viewing disobedience as a virtue, one cannot help but recognize the beauty that disobedience carries. There is beauty in learning and transforming, which is something that cannot be stressed enough.

What score would you give it? _____

Scores

Argumentative Essay #1 - score 6, 7

Argumentative Essay #2 - score 7, 8

Argumentative Essay #3 - score 6

A Final Word

Along with the AP course information already provided in this guide, here is the course schedule for my class. If you decide to use this Year at a Glance, you'll find the documents referenced below, enclosed in this book.

Week 1
- Syllabus
- Prepare students for class
- Review Summer Reading Thank You for Arguing
- Review AP exam and grading

Performance Task
Take Baseline: AP Lang. Secured Full Exam

Weeks 2-5
- Review: Details, Imagery, Syntax, Tone
- Review **A Word on Rhetorical Analysis**
- Review: Multiple Choice and Rhetorical Analysis results from the Baseline

Begin FRQ Essay Lessons
- First: Reading the Prompt
    o Prompt breakdown
    o Prompt sample FRQs
    o Prompt analysis of Rhetorical prompt
    o Review Prompt Analysis Questions
- Second: Reading the Text
    o Review Strategies and appeals
- Third: Writing the Essay

Begin with Puzzle Essays using:
    o Three Intros FRQs 2002, 2003, 2003 B
    o Two Bodies FRQs 2002, 2003 B
    o One Conclusion FRQ 2003 B

Performance Task
Take Practice Multiple Choice Exam

Week 6-10
- Review: Figurative Language – Metaphors, Similes, Personification, Hyperboles, Symbols and Irony.
- Review results of Multiple Choice Exam
- Review Multiple Choice testing strategies
- Student work:
    o   FRQ Practice Rhetorical Essays, 2004, 2004 B, 2004 B, 2005, 2006 B, 2008
    o   Present and review Rhetorical text in class and discuss it.
    o   Students begin writing response in class and finish it for homework.

Week 11-12
- Review: Diction, Details
- Review FRQ Synthesis results from Baseline
- Review the document **A Word on Synthesis**
Begin FRQ Essay Lessons
- First: Reading the Prompt
    o   Prompt breakdown
    o   Prompt sample 2017
- Second: Reading the Text
    o   Review Conversation with the Sources
- Third: Writing the Essay
o   Begin drafting a response to 2007 Art prompt
<u>Performance Task</u>
Compose Synthesis Essay

Weeks 13-15
- Review: Imagery, Syntax, Tone
- Student work:
    o   FRQ Practice Synthesis Essays, 2008, 2009, 2010 B
    o   Present and review synthesis texts in class and discuss them
    o   Students begin writing response in class and finish it for homework

Performance Task
Write to Synthesis and Rhetorical 2010 FRQs "Technology in the Classroom" and "Banneker."

Weeks 16-22
• Review: Figurative Language – Metaphors, Similes, Personification, Hyperboles, Symbols and Irony.
• Review results from Synthesis and Rhetorical 2010 FRQ
• Review student sample FRQs at different times
• Student Work: FRQ Practice Synthesis and Rhetorical essays:
    o 2011 Synthesis and Rhetorical
    o 2011 B Synthesis and Rhetorical
    o 2012 Synthesis and Rhetorical
• Review and discuss results of essays
Performance Task
Take AP Lang. Full Exam in class
• Week 19 and 20 Christmas Break.
• Review results of FRQs (only) after the break
Performance Task
FRQ Class Practice Synthesis and Rhetorical 2013

Weeks 22-25
• Review: Diction, Details, Imagery
• Review FRQ: Argumentative results from Baseline AP Lang. Full Exam
• Compare results and final AP score from first Full Exam to second Full Exam
• Discuss student progress
• Review Exam Multiple Choice results: Groups work on sections – 1, 2, 3, and 4
• Cover Multiple Choice strategies and test-taking techniques
• Review document **A Word on Argumentative**
Performance Task
Compose Argumentative essay: 2004 B "To belong"

Weeks 26-32
- Review: Imagery, Syntax, Tone
- Review student sample responses at different times

Performance Task
Take AP Lang. Full Exam. Full mock outside of class to allot for the 3 hours and 15 minutes. Saturday, in school. Begin FRQ Essay Lessons
- First: Reading the Prompt
    o Prompt sample 2004 B
- Second: Reading the Text
- Third: Writing the Essay
    o Begin writing in response to prompts:
    2005
    2006
    2009
- Review: Figurative Language – Metaphors, Similes, Personification, Hyperboles, Symbols and Irony.
- Review AP Lang. Full Exam
- Compare Baseline with the other Full Exam results
- Student work:
    o FRQ Practice Argumentative Essays, 2010, 2010 B

Performance Task
Take AP Lang. Full Exam in class. Full mock outside of class to allot for the 3 hours and 15 minutes. Saturday, in school.
- FRQ Practice Argumentative essays:
    o 2011 Argumentative
    o 2011 B Argumentative
    o 2012 Argumentative
    o 2013 Argumentative

Performance Task
2014 Complete FRQs (All 3 Questions)
- Review FRQ results and latest Full Exam results
- Week 32: Spring Break

Week 33-37
<u>Performance Task</u>
Take AP Lang. Full Exam. Full mock in of class, separated into different classes.
- Review results from Full Exam
- Compare results of Full Exams taken so far and AP Scores

<u>Performance Task</u>
Take AP Lang. Full Exam. Full mock in of class, separated into different classes.
- Class Practice:
    - Complete FRQs (all 3 questions):
        2015
        2016
        2017
- Exam Prep: review book handouts, as needed

Weeks 38-42
Early May AP College Board Exam
- AP Lit. Prep after the exam

Appendix

Writing Better Introductions

Original

The grim adventures Candide ventured through to find his loved one, Cunegonde, is representative of multiple life philosophies that Voltaire implemented in his book. Voltaire wrote this book and filled it with horror and humor to get his point across and teach a lesson on life. The long and extraneous path Candide took to be with Cunegonde can be compared to the saying "Rome was not built in a day." To find happiness and comfort his life, Candide had to experience getting beaten, war, the death of his friends, killing, robbery, and an earthquake. So, in order to marry and get with Cunegonde, he had get kicked out of Westphalia and take this long journey.

Revised

In Voltaire's novel, Candide's misadventures to find his beloved Cunegonde is representative of the long and extraneous path one must sometimes take to achieve fulfillment. This is akin to the quintessential axiom, "Rome was not built in a day." While the metaphorized "Rome" stands in for their relationship, and his worldly wanderings are a composite of the many "days" it takes to build something lasting and meaningful, Candide's happiness is directly proportional to the happenings of the novel. Essentially, he had to experience the days of torture, starvation, war, robbery, and the death of his friends to "build his Rome" with Cunegonde.

Original

In the novel Candide by Voltaire is written as a satire. This meaning that throughout the novel the author is mocking either an idea or a person and that is precisely what he does. He does mock just one idea but multiple. Some of the ideas he mocks is the idea of "beauty is in the eye of the beholder" and the style of romance as well as "it is what it is" and the idea that "everything happens for a reason". He does this by creating make up names and making a joke about everything as the novel is read.

Revised
Voltaire's Candide is a satiric indictment of people and philosophies. Clichéd, pseudo-philosophical phrases like, beauty is in the eye of the beholder undergo harsh criticism, as exemplified by Candide's failed romance with Cunegonde, whom he dislikes after she's lost her beauty. Other phrases, such as it is what it is, and everything happens for a reason, are respectively mocked for their laissez-faire and naïve approach to life. Essentially, these philosophies are scolded because they are empty and offer no significant improvement to anyone's personal life.

Writing Better Bodies

Original
Although the saying is not the only philosophies imbedded in the book, it could be interpreted as important in the role of Candide. "Rome was not built in a day" is supposed to mean that nothing was done quick or easy; it takes time and patience to get what you what. Candide dedicated his life to save and be with Cunegonde to the point where he stabbed her brother, and then sold him back to the gallery. He was willing to lose everything he had. He nearly lost his dear friend Pangloss to hanging and burning after an earthquake. But Pangloss' teaching allowed Candide to continue and find hope to rescue his love. His teaching was that everything happens for the best. Candide went through long heartbreaking moments but eventually got what he wanted because the saying indicated that being patient and putting the effort will have Rome built. Rome is representative his marriage to Cunegonde.

Revised
The saying is important to Candide's development because it intimates that nothing of enduring value is ever done quickly or achieved easily; it takes time and patience to create something worth loving. For example, Candide's devotion to Cunegonde drives him to killing a Jew and an Inquisitor to ensure her freedom, and even stabbing her brother, when he said they could not be together. His affection sees him through the loss of his mentor and friend, to hanging and burning after an earthquake – sees him through the loss of his wealth and the loss of his home. Candide's heartbreaks are a testimony to the power of resilience – to the many days it takes to build an everlasting Rome.

Original
First, the life philosophy having the courage to accept the things you cannot change and change the things you can't accept means that you shouldn't come with an excuse on something you can't change you have to own up to the fact that you can't change that situation that was inevitable and for the things you can't accept that can be changed change it one example of this is when Pangloss absurdly tries to explain how him getting Syphilis was a good thing because he says if people didn't have it they wouldn't have chocolate. Pangloss states "it was a thing unavoidable, a necessary ingredient in the best of worlds" (Voltaire 13). Pangloss needs to acknowledge the fact that him getting syphilis was very unfortunate and was not a good thing he should not just say it was for the best or for the greater good.

Revised
Some things cannot be changed, and that's that. In contrast, Pangloss' belief of living in the best of all possible worlds is not only naïve, but cowardly. It takes courage, humility, and a profound awareness of life to accept that we are powerless in the world. This acceptance is not to be conflated with surrender; some things can be changed, some things should

be changed. It is wisdom that tells us the difference. But some things, the novel implies, are beyond our abilities, our understanding and our control. For instance, when Pangloss explains to Candide that he contracted Syphilis, he depicts it as a good outcome, contending that if Columbus had not spread it, we wouldn't have chocolate. To him, "it is a thing unavoidable, a necessary ingredient in the best of worlds" (13), along with milk and flower, to make the necessary chocolate. If Pangloss was brave, he'd admit that needs to acknowledge the fact that him getting syphilis was very unfortunate and was not a good thing he should not just say it was for the best or for the greater good.

Writing Better Conclusions

Original
In the novel, society considers empathy to be its separating factor from androids and why humans see themselves as superior. Yet humans, like Rick, prove themselves to be hypocritical in that sense, as they feel that because they believe androids have no empathy, then it's justified to separate and retire them. But the importance of empathy itself shouldn't be measured by a test or the personalities adopted by others - Isidore shows that empathy is most powerful when one sees all life as equal and sacred.

Revised
In the novel, society considers empathy to be its separating factor from androids and why humans see themselves as superior. Yet humans, like Rick, prove themselves to be hypocritical, as they feel that because they believe androids have no empathy, then it's justified to separate and "retire" them. But the importance of empathy itself shouldn't be measured by a test or the personalities adopted by others – empathy, as Isidore shows us, is most powerful when one sees all life as equal and sacred.

Made in the USA
Middletown, DE
08 February 2019